Wicked RIDGEFIELD
CONNECTICUT

Wicked RIDGEFIELD CONNECTICUT

JACK SANDERS

THE
History
PRESS

Published by The History Press
Charleston, SC
www.historypress.net

First published 2016

Manufactured in the United States

ISBN 978.1.46713.682.2

Library of Congress Control Number: 2016941433

To the many police officers, local and state, who have nobly, caringly and effectively served Ridgefield over the past century.

Contents

ACKNOWLEDGEMENTS

S cores of people, many now gone, helped with the creation of this history. Special thanks to the following: Betsy Sheehan Reid of the Ridgefield Historical Society; Jennifer Adams Whelan of Dinand Library, Holy Cross College; Katherine Stewart of Senator Richard Blumenthal's staff; Chief John Roche of the Ridgefield Police Department; Allen Ramsey, assistant Connecticut state archivist; Thomas B. Nash of the *Ridgefield Press*; Jim Ferris; Cary Stone-Greenstein; Paul Hazel; Burt Kearns; Larry Fossi; and last, but not least, my wife, Sally Sanders, for her never-ending support and helpful suggestions.

INTRODUCTION

Wicked Ridgefield? What's with the "wicked"?

Local histories tend to focus not only on the major events in a community's past but also on the nicer ones. Any town's life, however, includes what might be called a wicked side—an assortment of bad guys or bad times that may include thievery, bigotry, murders, missing persons, arson and other assorted man-made misery. Often these people and events may have been forgotten because they were so long ago—or they may have been tucked away because people preferred to forget them.

This book describes aspects of Ridgefield's past that are sometimes tragic, often sad and occasionally mysterious. Many accounts provide glimpses into the lives that townspeople lived and trials they faced, while others recall crimes and criminals that upset those lives.

In many cases, however, the worst events can bring out the best in a community. People get together, stars emerge and improvements in how we function as a society result. This look at the darker side of Ridgefield history points out some heroes, offers some lessons and provides even a little humor. But let's face it, as anyone from Shakespeare to Agatha Christie could tell you, bad news make good stories.

Chapter 1

TIME FOR CRIME

B eing a generally well-to-do community, Ridgefield has been the target of robbers and thieves for more than a century. Some were better at their craft than others. And while most miscreants targeted cash, silver and jewelry, some even sought the lowly chicken.

THE CROOK WHO LOVED CORNED BEEF

For "Big Frank" Dreger, Ridgefield started out being just one stop on a long road of crime. However, his heist here helped prove his undoing, and with the aid of a corned beef dinner and a bottle or two of homebrew beer, he wound up spending the rest of his life in prison.

The story began on Thursday, February 23, 1933, when Upagenstit, the palatial mansion of Mrs. Frederic E. Lewis on West Lane, was broken into and silver worth more than $10,000 ($180,000 in today's money) was stolen.

"What adds mystery to the case is the fact that there were three dogs in the house at the time, and the servants' quarters were occupied," reported the following week's *Ridgefield Press*. Mrs. Lewis herself was at her New York City residence.

"It was a big case, a terrifying case for the people of Ridgefield and particularly the Lewis family," Leo F. Carroll recalled in a 1975 interview.

The burglary of Upagenstit off West Lane, a huge mansion, helped spell the downfall of "Big Frank" Dreger. *1920s postcard in author's collection.*

Carroll had been a lieutenant with the Connecticut State Police, assigned to the Ridgefield barracks, and had headed the investigation.

The silver-thieving spree continued down-county, with homes of the rich in Greenwich and Darien being hit. Finally, on the night of June 11, 1933, Darien police picked up two men carrying pillowcases filled with silver taken from a nearby mansion. One suspect was Frank Dreger, clearly the leader of the operation.

Despite being caught red-handed and undergoing hours of grilling, Dreger refused to cooperate with Darien police. Carroll told the story this way forty years later.

"One morning, a police officer over in Darien by the name of Amos Anderson phoned me and told me he had a silver thief he caught in his custody but couldn't get anything out of him. He knew I had this silver robbery, so he loaned him to me. I brought him to the Ridgefield barracks, and it just so happened that particular day we were having corned beef for dinner. This suspect smelled that corned beef cooking, and he asked me if it was corned beef. I said it was, and I said you're going to have some for dinner. But before you eat, you ought to cooperate with me and tell me something."

State police lieutenant Leo Carroll assisted a woman identifying silverware taken from her home in a 1939 case involving two hundred burglaries. *Author's collection.*

"Well," replied Dreger, "what do you want to know?"

Carroll described the Lewis estate burglary and asked whether Dreger was involved.

"Well, let me think it over—I don't want to talk too much," Dreger replied. "Are you going to take my fingerprints?"

Carroll said yes.

"Well, you'll find that I have a record, and you'll find that I've been a silver thief. But I want to think it over before I talk—but you say you're going to have me for a corned beef dinner?"

"I certainly am," replied Carroll.

"You know, I love corned beef, and if I could only have a bottle of beer, I might be able to help you," Dreger said.

Prohibition had not yet been repealed, and alcohol was, of course, never served at the state police barracks. However, said Carroll, "I went to a home brewery down the street and got a bottle of beer." (Some accounts say more than one bottle was acquired.)

"Well, that suspect after dinner took me for a ride up to a mountain in North Salem, and there, under a tree, were the empty silver sacks" from the Upagenstit heist.

———

A native of Hamburg, Germany, Frank Xavier Dreger was born in 1872, dropped out of high school after his first year and came to this country in 1894. He settled in New York City, worked as a cook and became a citizen in 1901. He married Emmy Hubner in 1902. By 1905, he was in prison at Auburn, New York, for an unspecified crime and was also there in 1925, according to census records. By 1920, his wife had died. The sixty-one-year-old had also done time in Sing Sing.

Dreger had spent most of his years outside prison as a burglar, specializing in silver. According to the *Press* account, no doubt based on information fed to it by Lieutenant Carroll, Dreger "has the appearance of a tramp" and "is known as the smartest silver thief in the United States.…The fact that Lt. Carroll and those who assisted him obtained his confession makes one of the biggest accomplishments of the State Police in years."

Dreger, the newspaper said, was "a very interesting personality. He has traveled extensively in Europe and his conversation appears to be very cultured. He is a man well along in years with a good constitution, born out by the fact that he has been shot three times and has suffered no after-effects."

He was good at what he did. All told, between February and June, Dreger had stolen silver in Ridgefield, Greenwich and Darien worth $150,000— that's about $2.7 million today.

Dreger told Carroll how he broke into Upagenstit. He had left New York with the intention of scouting out Ridgefield, "having heard a great deal about its wealth," the *Press* reported. Coming into town, he passed by the Lewis estate—a one-hundred-acre spread so elaborate it once had a staff of one hundred workers, including the family's own private physician; it seemed a likely candidate. He continued his journey to Danbury, returning here after dark and making arrangements with his partner, twenty-year-old Joseph Guarino, who remained in the car during the heist.

At the Lewis mansion, Dreger showed Carroll where he cut the glass of a side door to gain entry and how he made friends with the household dogs using some raw meat. He then reenacted his removal of the silver from a pantry and other locations. The burglary took nearly three hours to complete, he said.

What happened to the loot? A few pieces were recovered from Dreger's New York City apartment, but most of it had been melted down for sale—to the United States government for use in making coins!

Dreger pleaded guilty to the charges of burglary while armed and, in less than a week, had been sentenced to twelve to twenty years in prison at Wethersfield.

The burglary busts were not the end of Dreger's problems with the law, however. Police on Long Island noticed a similarity between him and Guarino and a pair of gangsters who were wanted for a bizarre murder two years earlier.

In what the *New York Times* called "an unprecedented story of piracy," an "old man and young man" in a canoe had boarded the cabin cruiser of Benjamin Collings on September 10, 1931, off Long Island. They beat up the thirty-eight-year-old Collings, a Dartmouth graduate marine engineer from Stamford, and then bound him and threw him overboard. Kidnapping his twenty-eight-year-old wife, Lillian, they paddled away in a canoe, leaving the Collingses' five-year-old daughter behind on the yacht. Mrs. Collings was abandoned on another motorboat moored offshore. She and the child were later found safe. Her husband's body eventually washed ashore on Long Island.

Man Resembles Collings Killer

One of two burglar suspects arrested in Darien, Conn., was partly identified by Mrs. Benjamin P. Collings of Stamford, Conn., as one of two men who in 1931 boarded their yacht in Long Island Sound and beat her husband to death. Frank Dreger, 61, (right), of New York, Mrs. Collings said, resembled the old man who boarded their boat. The man arrested with Dreger, Joseph Guarino, 20, (left), did not fit the description of the young man who figured in the Long Island Sound crime, Mrs. Collings said. Stephen Stanton, a state policeman, is standing behind the two suspects.

Frank Dreger (*right*) and accomplice Joseph Guarino (*left*) are shown in the old St. Petersburg, Florida *Evening Independent* in June 1933. *Google Newspaper Archives.*

The story made headlines across the country for days and continued to pop up again for several years as police came up with new suspects. Though it was nearly two years since the killing and kidnapping, a policeman noticed the similarity between Dreger and Guarino and the descriptions of the thugs who had killed Collings.

Dreger and Guarino were shown to Mrs. Collings, who spotted a resemblance between Dreger and the older attacker. Dreger denied any connection with the case and maintained he was in New York City on the night of the Collings attack.

"I would not kill anybody," Dreger told police. "I only steal from the rich."

Mrs. Collings was asked to look him over again the next day. When she viewed him the second time, she decided that Dreger was not one of the "pirates."

That brief episode of misidentification made headlines across the country—even the front page of the *Idaho Falls Post Register*.

Dreger never had another chance at his illicit craft of silver thievery—or to drink another beer. He died in the state prison in 1941 at the age of sixty-nine.

A MICKEY FOR JIMMY JOE

Robberies occurred occasionally in and about town, but only one involved a Mickey Finn, flappers and a man who became a Ridgefield legend.

On Friday, December 5, 1924, James "Jimmy Joe" Joseph was working at his small grocery store on the Danbury Turnpike, predecessor of today's Route 7, in Georgetown. A car carrying two young men and two young women pulled up. The *Ridgefield Press* described the women as being "of the flapper species."

The foursome seemed a friendly bunch, striking up what was later described as a "jolly" conversation with Jimmy Joe. Soon Ferris Hajjar, one of the men, pulled out a bottle of whiskey and offered Joseph a drink. "James is known as a man who never indulges in intoxicants and declined the invitation," the *Press* reported. Then one of the women produced a bottle of lemon soda, poured some in a cup and offered it to Jimmy Joe. He took a drink and, moments later, passed out. The quartet grabbed $135 (about $1,900 in today's dollars) and took off.

James Joseph was an old-fashioned success story, both in his life's work and his life's length. He died on March 6, 1972, and since his birth certificate said he was born on January 1, 1858, he was apparently 114 years old. He would have been around 68 when he was slipped the Mickey and robbed.

Born in Lebanon, then part of Syria, of an ancient Druze family, James Joseph came to the United States in 1903 and joined his brother, M.C. "Joe" Joseph, in operating a store in Danbury. They also sold fruit and vegetables on an auto delivery route through Ridgefield, which attracted them to the town. In 1918, Joe Joseph began operating Joe's Store near the corner of

James "Jimmy Joe" Joseph, who was drugged in a 1924 robbery, is shown at Joe's Store in the 1950s. Ridgefield Press *archives.*

Main Street and Danbury Road while Jimmy Joe opened a similar store in Georgetown. (The first Joe's Store in Ridgefield was in a brick building on Danbury Road that has been recently used as a candy shop. Soon, Joe Joseph moved to the corner of Main Street and North Salem Road in the building now occupied by Country Corners. To this day, this intersection is called Joe's Corner.)

In the early 1940s, Joe Joseph died, and Jimmy Joe took over the Ridgefield store. He became a citizen in 1958 but could not become a voter because he couldn't pass the literacy test—though he was well read in Arabic. When the Supreme Court banned literacy testing as a voting requirement in 1970, Jimmy Joe Joseph—well over one hundred years old and a resident for nearly seventy years—walked into the office of Town Clerk Ruth Hurzeler to be sworn in as a voter. "He had tears in his eyes," Hurzeler said later.

———

Arthur A. Smith, a carpenter who lived near the Georgetown store, drove by around four thirty that afternoon and saw Joseph "jollying" with a group of people. A little while later, Smith returned to do some shopping and found Joseph lying on the floor, unconscious. "Judging that the man was in serious condition, he telephoned to Dr. Charles Ryder, who quickly diagnosed the fact that the man was suffering from the effects of some powerful drug," the *Press* said. "He ordered his removal to his home where he was given constant attendance during the night, but he did not fully recover consciousness until a late hour Saturday morning."

Joseph did not see the car that carried the group of robbers, but he could give state police from Ridgefield a detailed description of the quartet. His information must have struck a spark of recognition in the officers, for by Saturday evening, Sergeant John Kelly and Officer Leo F. Carroll were in Danbury, rounding up the robbers. They first arrested Tony Howard, twenty-eight, proprietor of a "coffee house" on River Street in Danbury, who apparently told police the whereabouts of his accomplices. A little while later, Mrs. Gertrude Conners, twenty-nine; Miss Isabelle Chambers, twenty-three; and Hajjar, twenty-nine, all of Danbury, "were gathered in on the street," the *Press* said. Hajjar was described as the ringleader of the group. They were jailed after failing to post $2,000 bond each.

Wilton Town Hall, used as a courtroom, was packed on Monday, December 8, with friends and families of the Danbury suspects. Lawyers managed to get bond reduced to $1,000 for Connors and Howard, while Chambers had the bond lifted because, her lawyer maintained, she was in "ill health." Hajjar remained under $2,000 bond. The three were unable to post their bonds and were returned to the jail in Danbury. However, they soon managed to scrape together the money, made bond and were released.

"Jimmy Joseph is again able to conduct business at his grocery and is being congratulated by many friends and patrons, not only on his complete recovery from the effects of the drugs, but because he has recovered over $50 of the roll that afternoon," the *Press* said that week.

In early January before another large crowd in Wilton Town Hall, Hajjar and Connors pleaded guilty to theft, were fined $25.00 and costs of $92.01 each and got thirty-day suspended jail sentences. Chambers and Howard pleaded guilty to receiving stolen goods and were fined $15.00 and costs of $82.01 and given fifteen-day suspended sentences.

The sentences may have been suspended because the foursome had already spent time in jail. However, one wonders whether they would have gotten off so easily if the four had drugged and robbed one of the town fathers instead of a humble immigrant from the Middle East.

A RASCAL AT THE TAVERN

Scoundrels weren't all of modern vintage. In her diary, Anna Marie Resseguie, daughter of the innkeepers of the Keeler Tavern on Main Street, tells a strange tale of old-time fear and old-time justice.

On August 14, 1855, a man named Fisher arrived at the inn from Danbury, wishing to stay "a day or two." He apparently proclaimed himself to be a man of considerable wealth, Resseguie wrote.

Two days later, she reported, the man "purchases" the Main Street houses of Thomas Rockwell and Jesse Bradley. (Rockwell's place later became the Elms Inn, while the Bradley house, located where Ballard Park is now, had earlier been the home of Colonel Philip Burr Bradley, a prominent local citizen and Revolutionary War leader, and was later the home of music publisher Lucius H. Biglow and his daughter, Elizabeth Biglow Ballard.)

A man and a woman, both strange, visited the Resseguies' inn, now Keeler Tavern Museum, in August 1855. *Circa 1900 postcard in author's collection.*

The Resseguies were beginning to become suspicious of this "millionaire," as Anna called him.

Then, on the eighteenth, Anna wrote that "a girl came here last night, pretending to be on her way to Round Hill to teach school, and also to have been robbed. Her story seems improbable from her appearance and conversation before she goes to bed," Anna said.

Anna then revealed that because of the presence at the inn of both the girl and Fisher, she was "very much frightened in the night…Feel ourselves in awful company."

The next morning, innkeeper Abijah Resseguie told the young woman that he had looked into her story and found it "discredited." The girl promptly departed. Then, around noon, word came that Fisher was claiming to be ill and wanted to recuperate in his room at the inn. "Mother objects and doubts are entertained whether the sickness is real," Anna writes. Meanwhile, several Ridgefield men headed up to Danbury to look into Fisher's background.

Then, on the nineteenth, Anna reported, "our slumbers were disturbed between 3 and 4 this morning by the arrival of 12 men." The investigation of Fisher's past in Danbury had revealed "the man of fortune to be a rascal. The millionaire is dragged from his sick bed and paraded through the street." Fisher was then given a whipping—or, as Anna put it, "tanning"—and, with his hands secured behind him, was tied to a tree in front of the Rockwell place to be put on public display.

"He however made his escape this morning," Anna said.

Two days later, word came that "the villain" had been sighted in South Salem, but that, presumably, was the last Ridgefield ever heard of or from the "rascal"—or his possible female companion.

THE BANK BUNGLERS

Some burglars might be better classified as bunglers. Back in 1894, for instance, six bank robbers using dynamite more than literally "blew it."

Dr. George Lane, a dentist, and his wife were asleep around 2:00 a.m. in their apartment over the offices of the Ridgefield Savings Bank and the post office, which were then sharing the space where Deborah Ann's candy store is today on Main Street. Mrs. Lane was aroused by the sound of sawing below but decided it was Postmaster D. Smith Sholes doing some work.

Suddenly, an explosion rocked the apartment, which soon began filling with smoke. Mrs. Lane thought the building was on fire. She ran to the rear window and threw it open. The *Ridgefield Press* said she saw several men down below and, thinking they had responded to the fire, asked for help.

Perry's Market, now Deborah Ann's Sweet Shoppe, in the 1920s. In 1894, it was a bank where burglars blew up the safe. *Ridgefield Historical Society archives.*

That may not have been the wisest move. The men were members of the burglary gang, and one told her to shut the window or he would "blow her brains out."

She apparently didn't react quickly enough, for the man started firing a revolver at her, and one bullet grazed her cheek. "Then she fully realized her danger," the *Press* said, with perhaps a bit of understatement. "She called her husband and the cry of 'murder' and 'robbers' peeled [*sic*] forth, arousing the next door neighbors, who appeared outside." The *New York Times* said simply that she "cried lustily for help."

Those cries and the appearance of others awakened by the explosion apparently panicked the sextet, for they suddenly took off, leaving the contents of the bank's safe behind—even though they had successfully blown its door off. The safe contained $50 in cash and postage stamps; the bank also served as the village post office. That $50 is the equivalent of about $1,300 today.

The odd thing is, the attack on the bank seemed to have been carefully planned in advance. According to the *Times*, "Last week a stranger, who said he hailed from New York, applied at a local hotel for board. He said he had come to Ridgefield to recover his health. The new boarder had no apparent occupation, and, Postmaster Sholes now remembers, received no mail. As he has not been seen since the burglary, the people believe that he came here to plan the robbery and took an active part in carrying it out."

Sholes was both postmaster and the cashier for the bank. Postal valuables and bank deposits were kept together in the single safe. When Sholes accumulated more money than he thought safe for the safe, he took the surplus to Danbury to deposit in a big bank there, as there was no large bank with a vault in Ridgefield. However, three weeks later, the board of directors of the savings bank (now Fairfield County Bank) voted to buy a then-modern, burglar-proof safe equipped with a time lock.

The burglars also left their burglary tools behind, but it was little loss to them; the tools had been stolen from the nearby blacksmith shop of Albah Jerman. "With these they pried off the iron bars of the south rear window, twisting them in such a manner as to gain entrance," the *Press* reported. "The work throughout, the noise they made in sawing, etc., would indicate that the burglars were amateurs."

Amateurs or not, they were never caught.

CHICKENS A LA DICKENS

While cash, silver and jewelry were the target of most thieves who have hit Ridgefield, the foul burglars could also be fowl burglars. Two strange cases of the youthful chicken thieves harken back to characters in a Charles Dickens novel.

The first barnyard marauders, called at times the Howard-Reddy Gang, began making headlines in June 1924 when state police arrested three young men and fingered others. Fred Reddy, twenty-one; Peter Howard, seventeen; and Frank Cook, twenty-two, were described as part of a "gigantic chicken thieving ring" that had hit farms in Ridgefield and many other nearby Connecticut and New York towns over the previous ten years. Poultry worth hundreds of thousands of today's dollars was grabbed at night and then sold, still alive, in New York City.

The ringleader was Edward Howard, father of the seventeen-year-old Peter. Accounts in the *Ridgefield Press* described Edward as "the sinister stimulus of the obliquity of not only the three boys, including his own son, but of his wife, who, it was said, was bulldozed through fear of physical injury into assisting in achieving one of the most amazing theft plots uncovered in this stage for many years."

State police said Howard, from nearby Brewster, New York, drove around the Connecticut and New York countryside, "directing the schemes of the coop pillagers." His son was described as "lacking all his life proper parental guidance or the smallest semblance of an education" and, thanks to his father, "could not read or write a word of English." The boy had apparently been stealing chickens since he was eight or nine years old.

Howard and another adult named Benjamin DeNike were arrested by New York authorities and wound up in Sing Sing. The three young men arrested by state police sergeant John Kelly and Officer Leo F. Carroll were tried in this state and found guilty. But the judge decided to give Cook and Howard "a second chance" and did not send them to prison. Reddy, however, was a parole violator from the New York State prison at Elmira and was turned over to New York authorities. A New Canaan man named William Conklin was also arrested and convicted.

Fred Reddy, who had lived in Ridgefield, had apparently been close to Howard, leader in the gang, explaining why the state police called them the

Even chicken thieves were chased by state troopers, shown in the 1920s at East Ridge barracks, now Ridgefield police headquarters. *Joseph Hartmann photo,* Ridgefield Press *archives.*

Howard-Reddy Gang. And sure enough, after serving his time at Elmira, Reddy showed up several years later as one of a new gang of chicken thieves whose territory stretched throughout western Connecticut from Long Island Sound to the Massachusetts border.

This gang had an even more bizarre leader than the previous one.

In August 1930, Norwalk police arrested Fred and Samuel Reddy, Mrs. Ruth Jennings Reddy, Harold Coggswell, Benny Olmstead and Clarence Jennings Sr. and his son, Clarence Jr.

Police said Clarence Sr., the leader of the gang, beat his children—Junior and Mrs. Reddy—to force them into stealing chickens. Ruth Jennings Reddy told police that once when she had refused to participate in the thievery, her father had tied her thumbs to two spikes nailed over an open doorway and had left her suspended in the air with her toes barely touching the floor—

27

the weight of her body on her thumbs and toes. When she would cry out in pain, her father would beat her. The torture continued until she agreed to accompany him on poultry farm raids. She was eighteen at the time of her arrest, but the torture occurred when she was around sixteen. Clarence was sixteen when arrested.

How Mrs. Reddy was related to Fred Reddy is unclear. By the time she was eighteen, she had been married to and divorced from Warren Reddy, who died in 1930 when a tree fell on him in New Canaan. Warren and Samuel may have been Fred's brothers.

Most of the gang was sent to prison for up to four years. The children were given probation.

THE HORSE THIEF'S TWO RIDES

Chickens weren't the only animal objects of thieves a century or two ago. While cattle rustlers may have been rare in this neck of the woods, horse thieves weren't. One young man's decision to steal a bay back in 1907 led to his making a little bit of history in an unusual—and, for him, certainly undesired—way.

Arthur B. Cole was twenty years old and worked as the night watchman for B.E. Sperry's Livery Stable on Catoonah Street, across from where the Ridgefield firehouse is today. Sperry's was housed in a huge building and provided "room and board" for many village horses, as well as housed horses that could be borrowed like today's rent-a-cars.

On Thursday, August 22, Cole decided he needed money, and to get it, he'd steal a horse from the stable and sell it in Danbury. Sometime during Thursday night, Cole saddled a boarded horse and headed up to Danbury, where he sold the animal for $100 and promptly headed for a local bar.

Cole was apparently not the brightest candle in the stable. Though he did sneak the horse out a side door and through a neighbor's backyard, he apparently made little effort to hide his involvement in the theft. And it's unclear how he could have thought no one would have known he did the deed; the horses he took care of may have been smarter than he was.

Meanwhile, by dawn, Sperry discovered the horse missing, and based on reports of witnesses, Constable Frank Taylor telegraphed Danbury police: "Keep watch for a man riding a bay saddle horse which was stolen here early this morning. He is going toward Danbury." A description of Cole was included.

Arthur Cole stole Albert Wiggin's horse from Sperry's Livery Stable on Catoonah Street, opposite the firehouse. *Circa 1915 postcard in author's collection.*

A Danbury patrolman named Dougherty was assigned to the case and began making the rounds of the local saloons. When he walked into one dark and dingy establishment on Ives Street, "Cole, spotting him, endeavored to hide, but he was not quick enough to escape the hawk-eyed officer, who placed him under arrest and took him to the police station," the *Ridgefield Press* reported the next week.

Cole still had the $100 check, which he'd not had time to cash. The horse was recovered.

Constable Taylor and Sperry borrowed an automobile to go to Danbury to pick up Cole, who was later arraigned and failed to post $500 bond ($12,500 in today's dollars). The prisoner was then shipped off to the county jail in Bridgeport.

"Young Cole enjoys the distinction of being the first prisoner ever brought to Ridgefield in an automobile as well as the first ever taken to Bridgeport jail from here in the same manner," the *Press* reported. "It was also the occasion of Patrolman Dougherty's first ride in an auto."

THE THIEF'S SHADY VICTIM

The horse Arthur Cole decided to steal belonged to Albert H. Wiggin, who lived on nearby Peaceable Street. Though Wiggin was on the far opposite end of the social and economic scale from Cole, he was a man once investigated for shady dealings of his own.

A minister's son who was born in 1868 in Medford, Massachusetts, Wiggin became one of the world's leading bankers and was once listed among America's richest people. He was president of Chase National

Albert Wiggin (*left*) and J. Pierrepont Morgan (*center*) in New York City in 1917. Wiggin's behavior sparked a Senate investigation. *Library of Congress.*

Bank in New York, a post he assumed after A. Barton Hepburn, his predecessor who had a house on High Ridge, was run over by a bus on a New York City street.

Despite many good things he did for Chase, federal authorities later labeled Wiggin a scoundrel after it was revealed that, during the period of the crash of 1929, he had been selling short some forty thousand of his personal shares in Chase National Bank at the same time he was committing Chase's money to buying. He put his earnings in a Canadian holding company to avoid taxes and made millions that the bank itself did not discover until a later U.S. Senate investigation.

"This is like a boxer betting on his opponent—a serious conflict of interest," said financial reporter Andrew Beattie.

Ferdinand Pecora, chief counsel to the Senate Banking Committee, said of Wiggin: "In the entire investigation, it is doubtful if there was another instance of a corporate executive who so thoroughly and successfully used his official and fiduciary position, for private profit." Wiggin even made the cover of *Time* magazine in August 1931.

Economics professor and market historian Charles Geisst said what Wiggin did "gave banking and the stock market a bad name for at least two generations after the Crash."

Wiggin was forced to retire but was never prosecuted for any legal wrongdoing. He was given a $100,000-a-year pension from the bank

Albert Wiggin's house on Peaceable Street was one of the "longest" in town. Recent owners have reduced its size. *Postcard in author's collection.*

($1.7 million in 2016 dollars) but later turned it down after a widespread public outcry.

As a result of the case, Congress added the "Wiggin Provision" to the federal Securities Exchange Act to prevent company directors from selling short on their own stocks and making a profit from their own company's demise.

Later in life, Wiggin became a benefactor of many organizations. He donated a huge collection of prints to the Boston Public Library, the New York Public Library and the Baltimore Museum of Art. He contributed to the MIT library, endowed a scholarship at Middlebury College and created a foundation that contributed to many organizations.

A TOUGH TIME AT THE TONTINE

Allan Gerdau was a generous millionaire but an eccentric one who didn't care much about making money. Instead, he spent his years in pursuits so unusual and wide ranging that a relative once called him a "kook." One of his interests was collecting and selling art and antiques, and that led to the most costly crime in Ridgefield's history.

Gerdau, who lived in nearby West Redding, headed a New York City importing company that, among other things, was involved in a huge trove of giant pearls, cultivated off the shores of Australia and growing to the size of gumballs. He eventually became somewhat famous for his non-business activities, including taking out many large advertisements in the *New York Times* and other newspapers to offer his views on everything from the Vietnam War and striking air traffic controllers to South African apartheid. One ad offered his seven basic beliefs, which included, "We are not so stupid as to think we can have the blessings we want without sacrifice and work."

Gerdau was generous, often to people he did not know. He heavily tipped people who waited on him and once paid for a trip to India for a waiter he liked at a Manhattan restaurant so the man could visit his ailing parents. While dining at Stonehenge Inn in Ridgefield, he would often have bottles of champagne sent to "love birds" he saw in the dining room.

It was not unusual to spot Gerdau; his wife, Florence; and their four daughters riding around Redding and Ridgefield in a big Lincoln convertible, all loudly singing "You Are My Sunshine," said Stephen G. **Bloom in** *Tears of Mermaids: The Secret Story of Pearls.*

More for fun than for profit, Gerdau opened in the mid-1960s a gallery at his Manhattan offices in the historic Tontine Building on Wall Street, calling it The Tontine Emporium. There he sold an eclectic collection of exotic and antique wares, including French art, Chinese vases, African masks, duck decoys, old quilts, antique English furniture and Tiffany lamps. He served sherry and gin-and-orange at 11:30 a.m. every weekday free to anyone who happened by, the *Times* reported in a story that called the emporium "an oasis of charm" on Wall Street.

Gerdau seemed more interested in showing off the art and artifacts than selling them. "What we want people to learn is that our concentration is not on selling, but on giving a customer a chance to love something," he told the *Times*. "That's what's important to us. Look at all the silver. It's foolish to have it all over the place—it takes so much polishing. But isn't it pretty?"

With his health beginning to decline in the early 1970s, Gerdau moved the Tontine Emporium to a 1755 house on Route 7 in the Branchville section of Ridgefield. In those days, Route 7 from Norwalk north into Massachusetts was a famous antiques trail, and the Tontine Emporium became one of the top stops for higher-end purchasers. Most locals probably never set foot in the emporium, but almost everyone knew the place because each Christmas season, Gerdau decorated a one-hundred-foot-tall spruce out front with thousands of colored lights. The tree could be seen for quite some distance.

The Tontine Emporium housed many treasures. And at around 1:30 p.m. on Tuesday, May 18, 1976, two young men walked into the shop, handcuffed the manager and left with twelve signed Tiffany lamps and lampshades. The reported value was more than $200,000—over $820,000 today. A floor lamp alone was worth $115,000 in today's dollars. It was the largest loss in a robbery in Ridgefield's history.

The two men had entered the store and browsed for a few minutes before approaching Ina Coleman, manager and a partner with Gerdau. They introduced themselves as acquaintances of a Mr. Gold who had called the previous week about two Chippendale mirrors he had seen in the window. Mr. Gold had inquired about when the shop would be open and said he'd stop by on Tuesday.

The pair then said they wanted to place a fifty-dollar deposit on one of the mirrors but also asked about some early American duck decoys that they knew were in a basement room. Mrs. Coleman led them downstairs, where they grabbed her, handcuffed her arms behind her back and taped her mouth. She was told to sit on the floor and that if she remained quiet, she would not be hurt.

One man went upstairs to remove the lamps—or, in some cases, only the shades from lamps. The other man, who was described as "very courteous," stood watch over Mrs. Coleman. At one point he even suggested that she would be more comfortable if she moved over onto a nearby rug.

The men left within fifteen minutes in what was thought to be a cream-colored station wagon with New York State plates.

Still cuffed, Mrs. Coleman managed to get up, climb the stairs and walk to a nearby shop where a merchant called police. Responding Ridgefield officers found Mrs. Coleman shaken up, with a minor injury to her face from either the tape or from falling down. Oddly enough, her handcuffs were the same kind used by the Ridgefield police, and their key was able to unlock them.

Gerdau told a *Ridgefield Press* reporter that the stolen lamps and shades were among the finest examples of signed Tiffany work. Besides the large peony floor lamp, a table lamp with a green dragonfly design of fractured glass was said to be "very rare" and worth $22,000 then (around $90,000 today). A very large tulip lamp was valued at $23,000, and a shade with a poppy design was $22,000.

Both police detectives and Gerdau believed that at least one of the men had been in the store before and knew exactly what they wanted. Only the Tiffany items were taken; vases and other antiques worth thousands of dollars each were left untouched. The stolen Tiffanys were never recovered.

Gerdau died in 1986 at the age of eighty-seven. His eight-paragraph obituary in the *Times* mentioned his career only in passing, focusing instead on the many advertisements he placed in that newspaper dealing with a variety of public issues and costing as much as $3,400 ($24,000 today).

"I'm not a flag-waving person, but sometimes one just has to stand up," he told the *Times* in 1967.

The eighteenth-century building that housed the Tontine Emporium was torn down a few years later to make way for a shopping plaza. With it went the tree that had once been a Yuletide landmark for many thousands of people who traveled U.S. Route 7.

Chapter 2

MURDER MOST FOUL

N o community can escape the worst of crimes, and Ridgefield and its people have had a share of involvement in murder and murderers.

THE FARMINGVILLE BONES

The macabre discovery in a Farmingville field on August 28, 1940, gave rise to one of Ridgefield's greatest mysteries, a crime that has remained unsolved for three-quarters of a century.

As workmen for Outpost Nurseries began digging up a four-year-old tree that was to be used for a landscaping project, a shovel unearthed a human skull. Police were summoned, but the discovery was kept secret until two weeks later when the *Ridgefield Press* revealed that "the skeletonic remains of a woman who apparently met a violent death a decade or so ago" had been uncovered.

The bones in a shallow grave brought back recollections of strange events years earlier, but a man who probed the secrets of those bones was soon dead himself.

Above: Cows roamed a field on David Jones's farm around 1900, near where the skeleton of a murdered woman was later found. Ridgefield Press *archives*.

Left: Dr. Harry Burr Ferris of Yale helped Lieutenant Leo Carroll with the mysterious skeleton but died before the investigation was completed. *Courtesy of James G. Ferris*.

Back then, the Connecticut State Police handled Ridgefield's criminal cases, which were few; the state police barracks on East Ridge is now the headquarters of the Ridgefield Police Department. Led by the colorful lieutenant Leo F. Carroll, investigators descended on the Farmingville scene and began scores of interviews with people in the neighborhood.

The site was atop a ridge on former pasture, once part of David L. Jones's Walnut Grove Farm—now the area of the Walnut Grove subdivision. Outpost Nurseries, a huge operation covering nearly two thousand acres in northeastern Ridgefield and nearby Danbury, had bought the land to plant nursery stock a few years earlier.

"News of the discovery was withheld at the request of the police until the bones had been examined by an anthropologist," the *Press* reported. That expert was Dr. Harry Burr Ferris, retired member of the anatomical department of Yale University and past president of the Connecticut Medical Association. Lieutenant Carroll had sought his advice in the past.

In his report, Dr. Ferris said the bones belonged to a woman between the ages of twenty-six and forty who was five feet four and one-half inches tall. "It is estimated that the skeleton had been in the ground for 10 years," the news story said. "It was found in a limestone composition soil which probably hastened decomposition."

The skull had been fractured, violently.

"We have some interesting clues and are progressing slowly, steadily and surely," said a confident-sounding Lieutenant Carroll.

The state police's own records may have offered a clue as to the date of the crime. Back on June 30, 1930, several people in Farmingville "were aroused in the night by the screams of a woman," the *Press* account reported. "Some insisted the woman was being murdered."

Perhaps with a tad of understatement, the newspaper added, "This incident may have had something to do with the skeleton just found."

Three weeks after the discovery, the state police were also checking a report that "a couple who formerly lived not far from the spot where the skeleton was found, mysteriously disappeared several years ago."

Then, on October 12, state police learned that Dr. Ferris, their key expert in the investigation, had himself died—of natural causes.

By late October, investigators were claiming, "many important clues have yet to be checked." But three-quarters of a century later, the case of the Farmingville bones remains a mystery. And like the physician who studied the bones, everyone who was involved in the investigation is now dead.

LOVE, HATE AND A HERMIT

Diamonds may be a girl's best friend, but they spelled the downfall for a young Danbury man in a tale that one newspaper headlined, "Love and Hate Prompt Farmhand to Murder Hermit." The sensational and often weird crime was later called "my most exciting case" by the man who solved it—the head of the Connecticut State Police.

John C. Kelly considered solving the "hermit's murder" his most exciting case. Ridgefield Press *archives*.

The gruesome story came to light on Saturday, May 5, 1923, when the cottage of a recluse farmworker was found burned to the ground off Simpaug Turnpike on the Ridgefield-Redding town line. There was evidence of foul play and no signs of the occupant.

Sergeant John C. Kelly, commander of the state police barracks in Ridgefield, was called to investigate. He was met by John Dandone and Albert Aigner, who took him to the scene. "Aigner showed me a man's vest which was lying on the roadside," Kelly recalled thirty years later. "The vest was covered with blood, and Aigner identified it as belonging to George Hultz, who lived in the house which burned down during the night."

Kelly was no ordinary policeman. He went on to become the commissioner—the chief—of the entire Connecticut State Police Department. In a 1955 reminiscence in the *Bridgeport Herald*, he called this his "most exciting case." One reason may have been that veteran police officers were telling him he was pursuing the wrong paths in the investigation.

Another reason may have been the brashness of the murderer—one of the two men who had showed him the crime scene.

John Dandone or Dondone—his name was spelled both ways in accounts of the case—was born around 1899 in Italy. He came to this country in 1918 and worked as a laborer on farms in the Topstone neighborhood of western Redding and eastern Ridgefield. Often, he was hired as a seasonal worker, as was George Hultz. In fact, Hultz and Dandone often labored together, and according to contemporary accounts, Hultz frequently harassed Dandone and teased him, probably about his Italian accent and manners.

Dandone had a way with words. He was known as a smooth talker in the Italian American community of Danbury. He even convinced some that he was a special agent for the state police. At one point he was showing up at speakeasies in Danbury, identifying himself as a state policeman working undercover and demanding "hush money" to keep quiet.

But Dandone also was known for having a temper.

Sergeant Kelly examined the ashes of the shack. He found the remains of a shotgun and, in its barrel, one shell that had been discharged.

Outside, "I found an impression in the ground that looked like a man's head had been driven into the ground with considerable force," Kelly recalled. "The ground was stained with blood at this spot." He followed a trail in the grass that looked as if something had been dragged. The trail crossed Simpaug Turnpike and the Danbury-Norwalk railroad tracks to the shore of Umpawaug Pond.

"A rowboat was beached near the end of the trail," Kelly said. "It could be seen that someone had been in the boat during the night as a large print was on the seat of the boat, indicating someone had sat down on it. The prints were made by dew settling on the seat of the board during the night."

A team of professional draggers was hired to search the pond for the body, but after several days, nothing was found. Kelly did not give up. He asked four constables from New Milford, who were skilled at dragging for bodies in the Housatonic River, to volunteer their services, and using a special grappling hook, they soon found the corpse. Hultz's body was brought to the temporary vault at Branchville Cemetery and examined. An autopsy established that a blow in the face with a blunt instrument killed him. His lungs contained no water, and no alcohol was in his stomach, the *Press* said. "This would show that no drunken brawl preceded the slaying."

The *Press* added, "It is thought robbery was the motive as Hultz was known to have had about $200 which he carried around." What's more, the farmhand had just been paid that day. When the remains were pulled up, a watch was found in his pocket, the newspaper said.

Hultz and his wife were divorced and had a child. "He was estranged from both," the *Press* said, adding that the owner of the estate on which Hultz lived—Mrs. A.K. Van Rein of Brooklyn, New York—said she would cover the cost of the funeral.

Dandone had told Sergeant Kelly he had seen Hultz standing in the doorway of his shack as he passed by to pick dandelion greens in a nearby meadow. Dandone said he had returned home, cooked and ate the greens and gone to bed.

Sergeant Kelly found something strange about Dandone and his dandelion story and decided to look into the background of the twenty-four-year-old.

One of eight children, John Cornelius Kelly was born in Ridgefield in 1885. When World War I broke out, he enlisted in the navy and served on submarine chasers. Around 1920, he joined the state motor vehicle patrol, a motorcycle unit that in 1921 became part of the Connecticut State Police.

He was quickly recognized as a leader, and in 1922, he was promoted to sergeant and given command of the new Ridgefield barracks.

Kelly's pursuit of Dandone began with talking to people who knew the man. He learned that Dandone had a girlfriend who had recently arrived from Italy and that he had proposed marriage to her. Dandone had told the girl's brother and other family members that he had more than $7,000 in the bank.

"Dandone had told his sweetheart, her brother and their friends that he was a special state policeman secretly appointed to solve the case," Kelly said. "He gloated over the failure of the police to break the case. He said the 'dumb cops' at the barracks didn't know he was a special cop. He even went to see Hultz's wife to express his sympathy and promise that he would find the foul killer."

The girlfriend's brother began to wonder about Dandone's intentions, including the lack of an engagement ring. The brother later told Kelly that he had warned Dandone: "I told you when you first started to go with my sister that it would be all right if you married my sister, but if you tried to fool me like you fooled somebody else, you better look out!"

Under pressure, Dandone went to Mason & Grime's Jewelry Store in Danbury and bought a diamond ring for $100—the equivalent of $1,400 in today's money—using $10 and $20 bills. However, Kelly had established that just before the murder, Dandone had no money, had been borrowing from friends and his salary was only $15 a week.

"I suspected Dandone had two reasons for killing Hultz," Kelly wrote in 1955. "One was that Dandone did not like Hultz because the hermit always teased Dandone. The other was that Dandone needed money" to buy the ring.

Kelly took Dandone to the morgue and made him look at Hultz's body. "He didn't show a trace of troubled conscience," Kelly said.

He then began questioning how a $15-a-week farmhand could afford a $100 diamond ring, especially when he had been so broke that he had been borrowing from others. "He couldn't think of an alibi to explain how he came by the money," Kelly said. "I had him trapped and he knew it. He then blurted out that he took the money from Hultz after killing him in the shack."

But Dandone maintained the killing was in self-defense.

Dandone told Kelly that he had been walking down the tracks to pick dandelions for dinner. As he neared Hultz's shack, the hermit came out on the front porch and fired a shotgun at him. Angered by the shot, Dandone said he ran to the shack and began fighting with the seventy-two-year-old hermit. During the fight, he grabbed the shotgun and struck Hultz in the head, he said. In the struggle, he added, the stove overturned, setting fire to the building.

"Hultz tried to shoot me!" Dandone told Kelly. "So I grabbed the gun and shot and battered the old hermit."

Neither the police nor the court believed Dandone's version. They questioned why someone who was being shot at would run toward the shooter instead of running away to seek safety. They also had testimony that Dandone was seen earlier walking toward the shack with a large bar of some sort. The state police later determined it was a log-pike, a wood-handled device used to grasp and move logs. They argued he planned to rob and kill Hultz to pay for the diamond ring.

Police also maintained that the shack was deliberately set afire to cover up evidence and perhaps make it seem that Hultz had perished in the blaze.

Dandone was charged with first-degree murder. The *Press* also reported that Dandone was suspected of being a night burglar. Police, the newspaper said, "believe him responsible for a number of robberies of summer cottages in this section, but in view of the seriousness of the offense with which he is now awaiting trial, it is not likely that they will press additional charges against him."

At the September trial, Dandone pleaded guilty to manslaughter and was sentenced to twelve to fifteen years in the state prison in Wethersfield. He was released in 1932 and, on December 9 of that year, deported to his native Italy.

———

"The crime to which Dandone confessed goes on record as one of the most baffling with which the authorities in this section of the state have had to deal in many years," the *Press* said. Then, in an elaborately constructed, ninety-one-word sentence, the newspaper added:

> *The amazing reserve with which Dandone had unflinchingly faced suspicions directed at him shortly after the murder, the callousness that permitted his pursuing his ordinary work-a-day affairs in the very neighborhood where*

he had killed a man with fiendish savagery not surpassed in Connecticut criminal history, and the extraordinary braggadocio that prompted him, the murderer, to masquerade covertly as a "special investigator" of the state police department and interview sundry persons pretending a public-spirited desire to unravel the terrible secret that was known to no man but himself, all collapsed.

And the newspaper heaped praise on Sergeant Kelly, whom it had recently indirectly criticized for his department's handing of a racial incident in town (see page 82).

"The credit of John Dandone's arrest is really due to the untiring efforts of State Policeman John Kelly," the newspaper said. "When Hultz's disappearance was first discovered, Officer Kelly promptly responded and investigated the matter. From his personal observations he deducted that a murder had been committed, which subsequent events proved to be correct. Officer Kelly formed his own theory as to the identity of the perpetrator, and was discouraged by older heads who thought the officer was wrong."

In 1945, John Kelly was made a major and executive officer of the state police department, and four years later, he was named chairman of the State Liquor Control Commission. In 1953, Governor John Lodge appointed him commissioner of the Connecticut State Police, a command he held until 1955. He might have held the office longer, but Kelly was a Republican and by then the governor, who made the appointments, was Abraham Ribicoff, a Democrat.

After his retirement, Kelly became a state representative from Ridgefield to the legislature. After that, he worked as a legislative consultant until he was eighty-two. He died in 1984 at the age of eighty-eight, still living in the town in which he was born.

THE MILL POND MURDER

Crimes involving Ridgefield sometimes went far beyond the borders of the town. In 1912, it took one of New York City's most famous detectives to solve a murder whose victim ended up in Georgetown by way of Branchville.

November 9 that year was a fine Saturday morning in town. Down in Georgetown, at the southeast corner of Branchville, several boys were playing along the shore of the large millpond that served the Gilbert and

NYPD deputy chief George Dougherty, shown around 1913, was a celebrity among detectives and wouldn't give up on the Mill Pond Murder. *Wikimedia Commons.*

Bennett wire factory. One of the boys happened to look out across the water and spot what seemed to be a large box floating on the surface.

"What's that?" they all wondered.

The boys grabbed a nearby dingy and rowed out to investigate. They found a trunk, wrapped in rope, and decided to tow it ashore. Cutting the rope and prying open the lid, the boys found the body of a woman. Her head bore strange wounds.

Thus began weeks of sensational news stories and months of investigations across two states and two continents. The accounts at first filled many columns of newsprint. But like so many other stories that were sensational at the outset, this one petered out in the eyes of the editors of the day. But not in the eyes of George Dougherty, the "burly, genial-faced" deputy commissioner and chief of detectives of the New York City Police Department.

The crime quickly became known as the Mill Pond Murder, and early theories as to a motive for the killing ranged from white slavery to illegal liquor sales.

Two days after the body was discovered, the *New York Times* was reporting that United States Secret Service agents had descended on Branchville and Georgetown. Officials, it seems, believed "the victim was slain because it was thought she was a government spy investigating white slave conditions."

That case involved women being brought to this country to serve as cheap labor or as prostitutes. Just two weeks earlier, Jennie Cavaglieri, "a white slave witness," had been lured into an automobile by five men and shot dead in Stratford, the *Times* reported.

However, a state prosecutor in Danbury with the strangely appropriate name of Beers felt the woman might have been murdered because she made revelations to the state police that led to "wholesale liquor raids here recently." He even theorized that the woman had been killed by being stabbed in the head with a stiletto while she was asleep.

The *Brooklyn Daily Eagle* reported at the same time that "the murder may have been committed somewhere else, possibly across the line in New York State, the body being brought here by automobile and thrown into the pond, but it is considered more probable that the murder was committed in Branchville or Ridgefield, or some other place near Georgetown."

There was even a theory that the woman was a victim of a double murder in Lewisboro, New York, just west of Ridgefield, where a man and wife, said to be selling illegal liquor, had suddenly disappeared two weeks earlier.

The theories were all wrong—except the thought that the crime was committed in New York State.

Headlines began to reflect the state of the stymied investigators: "Vainly Seek Clue to Pond Victim" (*New York Times*, November 11), "Mill Pond Murder Still a Mystery" (*Times*, November 12), "Georgetown Crime Is Yet Unsolved" (*Brooklyn Eagle*, November 11), "Still Some Doubt About Identity" (*New London Day*, November 14). But one headline suggested a strange and new twist in the case: "Faints Viewing Pond Victim."

The November 14 *Times* reported that some investigators suspected the victim was Grace Carbone of New Haven, and, the newspaper said, "police brought a strange woman in black from that city today. Accompanied by State Policeman Frank Virelli and Detective Michelli of the Homicide Bureau of New York City, the woman was taken to the vault in the Branchville

Cemetery, and collapsed when she saw the face of the dead woman. She was hurried from the vault in an automobile."

Nothing more was ever reported about the woman, why she fainted or what she told police afterward.

Meanwhile, the story said, Detective Michelli had discovered that a trunk, similar to the one containing the body, had been shipped to "the Yellow House" in Branchville. The Yellow House was a well-known boardinghouse used by many Italians who had recently immigrated to this country. Michelli also found Carlo Faro, who had boarded at the Yellow House, and, the *Times* said, Faro had provided "some useful information" to the police. "He was thoroughly terrorized and was hardly able to speak. He wished to escape from Branchville, and feared for his life if he talked of the case," the article said. "Faro stated that he saw the trunk delivered at the Yellow House, and positively identified the younger of the two men who dragged the trunk from the Georgetown Station as Salvatore Toredo. This man, Faro said, had been living in Branchville until recently and moved from there to New York."

Deputy Commissioner Dougherty had read the reports of the body found in a small Connecticut town. According to George Dilnot, author of the 1929 book *Triumphs of Detection: A Book about Detectives*, "Call it instinct, intuition, reasoning, what you will—he visualized a cleverly planned murder which had taken place, not in Connecticut, but in New York, many miles away."

And Dougherty set about solving the crime, with the help of a team of officers including Detective Michelli.

Born in 1865, George Samuel Dougherty was a former top agent with the famous Pinkerton Detective Agency. In 1911, the New York Police Department hired him as deputy police commissioner and head of the detective bureau in an effort to shake up and improve the bureau. A strict disciplinarian, he fought both criminals and men within his own department and became widely known for his police work.

Dougherty believed in using publicity, albeit discreetly, in his investigations. With his help, the Mill Pond Murder drew national attention as he circulated pictures and descriptions of the victim. "Dougherty even went to the length of enlisting the aid of the churches and schools in the attempt at identification," wrote Dilnot. Yet no one came forward with the victim's name.

Branchville Station around 1905. A body in a trunk arrived here in the fall of 1912. *Postcard in author's collection.*

Since a trunk was involved, he told his men to "investigate every railroad and trolley station, every expressman, or any person who had a vehicle of any kind for hire or loan."

That paid off. Detective Michelli found a station agent in Branchville who remembered the arrival of the trunk. Howard L. Lockwood, the agent aboard the express rail car from South Norwalk to Branchville, recalled the trunk and said that it "emitted a terrible odor, and that all in the car remarked it." At the Branchville depot, it was learned, an older, gray-haired man and two younger men, all with Italian accents, had put the trunk on a wheelbarrow and headed off.

Meanwhile, a detective in the city found a dealer in secondhand goods who'd sold a similar trunk to a tall Italian man with gray hair. The dealer remembered delivering it to a flat in a tenement in the Corcoran's Roost section of lower Manhattan, which was considered a "tough neighborhood" of its time. Commissioner Dougherty himself interviewed the tenement's elderly Irish landlady, who reported that the now-empty flat had been occupied by an older man, his wife, two young men and a girl, whose names she couldn't recall. Her description of the wife matched the victim in the trunk, and the older man resembled the fellow who had picked up the trunk in Branchville.

A search of the apartment uncovered bloodstained nails and a hammer, apparently used to inflict the wounds to the woman's head. Dougherty also found a dirty linen collar bearing the laundry mark "0.172." Days more of investigation revealed the collar had belonged to a well-to-do olive oil merchant.

Dougherty showed the merchant a picture of the victim. He recognized her immediately as Marie Geracci. She and her husband, Salvatore Geracci, had come from the merchant's native village in Italy. He even knew many members of the Geracci family on both sides of the Atlantic. The two men and the girl in the flat were nephews and a niece of Geracci, who was variously known as a tailor, wine seller and fruit vendor. The olive oil merchant said he didn't know how his collar had wound up in their apartment.

So now Dougherty had names and descriptions. However, Geracci and his relatives had disappeared.

Dougherty suspected the family might have fled to Italy. He contacted Italian authorities, who soon tracked down the two nephews and niece, arresting all three for complicity in the murder. But there was no sign in Italy of Salvatore Geracci himself.

Italian authorities did not extradite their suspects to America and opted to try the three relatives themselves. Under questioning, they broke down and confessed. Copies of the confessions were sent to the NYPD.

According to their account, Salvatore and Marie had a fierce quarrel late one night. The nephews tried to intervene but were chased away. "Crouched shuddering against the wall, they beheld all the terrible business of the murder," reported Dilnot. "Then, when it was over, the frenzied man, of whom they seemed to stand in abject fear, forced them to help him pack the body in a trunk," which was shipped to Branchville, a place Geracci was familiar with from visits in the past. They wheelbarrowed the trunk to the Yellow House and then to the pond where they attempted to sink it by attaching heavy railway "fishplates," the steel bars used to join rails.

Soon after, the nephews and niece fled the country, taking a ship to Naples. They were convicted of complicity and sentenced to prison terms.

Dougherty ordered a widespread search for Geracci. Law enforcement agencies here and abroad were given descriptions of the man. It was Italian police who received a tip that Geracci was hiding in Buffalo, New York. A short while later, on March 24, 1913, Geracci was arrested and brought back to New York. During questioning, he suddenly dropped to his knees, pulled out a crucifix, held it in the air and confessed to murdering his wife.

What led to the fatal quarrel?

Salvatore and Marie had grown up together in an Italian village where their fathers owned adjoining vineyards. The two fell in love and were married. But then one day, Marie disappeared. Salvatore learned that she had gone to America with a lover. "With murder in his heart, he sailed for New York," Dilnot reported. His nephews joined him later.

It took a while, but Geracci eventually located his wife with her lover—the very same olive oil merchant who had identified her picture for police. "I was going to kill her on the spot," Geracci told police. "But my love for her was too great. Instead, I embraced her and begged that we should again live happily together. She agreed, if I would spare her lover's life. To this I consented."

As Marie was packing her clothes in her lover's house, she apparently accidentally picked up one of his collars—the one that got left behind in the Corcoran's Roost flat.

The reunited couple seemed happy for a while, but Marie reportedly soon regretted losing the material comforts that her wealthy lover had provided. According to Dilnot's account, the end came when "she taunted her husband, and all his jealous suspicions were reawakened. One night he accused her of resuming clandestine meetings with her lover. For answer she spat in his face, the unforgivable insult to an Italian, and the maddened man choked her to death before the affrighted eyes of his relatives."

Geracci was convicted of second-degree murder and sentenced on May 13, 1913, to spend the rest of his life in prison. Eight months later, Dougherty was gone from the department, retiring to join his brother in running a detective agency. He eventually also taught in a police detective school, wrote books and hung out with the likes of Sir Arthur Conan Doyle.

When he died in 1931, the *Times* called Dougherty "one of the leading American detectives. In his long career he apprehended many dangerous criminals."

Dougherty was also a colorful and opinionated fellow, advocating the deportation of aliens after conviction for a crime, federal legislation to totally eliminate revolvers, the payment of rewards to the killers of hold-up men and the restoration of the whipping post as punishment for first offenders.

THE INFAMOUS FARRUGGIOS

The early '30s was a wild time on the national scene. Prohibition had created crimes and criminals, murders were commonplace and the Depression was sparking social unrest.

Involved in all of these problems were three brothers—Sam, Joseph and Calogero Farruggio—who spent their childhood in Ridgefield. In May 1934, two of the brothers made the news: "Desperate Man Hunt Centers in Ridgefield for Alleged Murderers of New York Cop," screamed the headline in the May 10 *Ridgefield Press*. In the *New York Times*, it was "2 Fanatics Named as Police Slayers." On their way to burn down a church, Sam and Joseph Farruggio had shot and killed a New York City policeman and a passerby and seriously wounded another officer.

The shootings occurred on Friday, May 4, around 3:00 a.m., when the Farruggios were stopped by Patrolmen Lawrence Ward and William Brennan as the brothers were walking on East 101st Street in Harlem. According to police, the two were on their way to "burn the first Roman Catholic Church they came to." One brother was carrying a two-gallon can of gasoline.

When the patrolmen tried to question the pair, they ran into a building at 322 East 101st Street where they lived with their other brother, Calogero, and "their aged mother."

Calogero was on the stoop, and Officer Brennan held him outside the building while Officer Ward chased the other two brothers. A shot rang out. Ward was hit in the shoulder and fell backward down a staircase, breaking his back. He died shortly afterward. Brennan released Calogero and chased Sam and Joseph up the stairs, over a rooftop, onto another building, down the stairs, out a door and down a street. The Farruggios began shooting; one bullet hit and killed bystander Ernest Krahenbuehl, whom the brothers apparently mistook for a detective, and another shot felled Officer Brennan, who was seriously injured but survived.

Sam and Joseph escaped, prompting the manhunt in New York City and Fairfield County. Calogero was held in jail as a material witness.

Hundreds attended the funeral of Officer Ward, who had been married only three weeks earlier. The *Times* described his widow weeping as the coffin was carried into the church, and the police band played "Nearer My God to Thee."

The *Press* story reported that two New York detectives were working with Lieutenant Leo F. Carroll, head of the state police in Ridgefield, in trying to track down the brothers. The two were "well known to Lt. Carroll" and were "said to be religious and social fanatics." The *Times* quoted New York Police captain Edward Mullins of the homicide squad as saying they were "inflamed by Communist literature and atheist pamphlets."

Captain Mullins said, "It was plain from Calogero's story that the brothers were obsessed with the idea that they were haunted by 'evil spirits' and that the only way they could rid themselves of the spirits would be by setting fire to a church—any church."

Police were checking out the pair's former haunts in both Ridgefield and Bridgeport. They were aided by information provided by Calogero, whom detectives described as "dull-eyed and not overly bright."

Some six months later, on January 18, 1935, two New York City transit policemen picked up "several suspicious-appearing individuals on the Astoria elevated line," the *Brooklyn Daily Eagle* reported on January 20. They included the Farruggios, who were "carrying brown paper bags which, they said, contained bread....As they were led to a patrol wagon by Patrolman Thomas Connors, they ripped the bags open, and drew revolvers from them. Firing away, they fled down a Brooklyn street. Police returned the fire and the pair dropped. They were taken to St. Johns Hospital, where they died."

Leo Carroll, shown in the 1950s, tried to track down the Farruggio brothers, murderers who grew up in town. Ridgefield Press *archives*.

The *Eagle*'s account was buried at the end of a long story that recounted six murders and shootings over the previous day or two in New York City.

———

The origin of the Farruggio brothers (also spelled Farruggia) is unclear. The *Times* said they were the only surviving offspring in a family that once numbered twenty-four children and that they came from "a remote corner" of Sicily. Citing Connecticut State Police, the *Times* said they had entered the country without passports.

However, in Ridgefield Town Hall are birth records that indicate the Farruggios were both born in Ridgefield—Salvatore "Sam" Farruggio in 1913 and his brother Giuseppe Liopoldo "Joseph" Farruggio three years later. They were listed as the sixth and seventh children of Calogero and Cyrenna Norata Farruggio, who, the records said, had come to this country from Parma, Italy. Calogero, the father, was listed on both birth certificates as a laborer.

Adding to the mystery is the fact that the birth records appear to have been supplied by the Connecticut State Police sometime after Sam and Joseph were killed. What's more, the birth years appear to conflict with the ages published in the *Times*, which had said Sam was forty and Joseph forty-two.

State police described Joseph as a "transient factory worker who settled down in Ridgefield as a small-time merchant and bootlegger" who had operated "an alcohol cutting plant." Salvatore, they said, "is a similar cut from the same cheese. He beat the war cloud out of Italy."

The *Times* said that Joseph and Salvatore had been arrested in Ridgefield in 1931 on a charge of receiving stolen goods and were sentenced to one to three years in state prison. "Their Ridgefield job was bad," Captain Mullins said. "It wasn't professional. They're not too sharp. It was the only crime on their record."

After they moved to New York City, police said, the brothers eked out a living peddling hot dogs from a hand cart along Third Avenue. Calogero did most of the work, with Sam and Joseph helping out.

"They seldom made more than 35 or 50 cents a day," the *Times* quoted police as saying.

THE MIMOSA MYSTERY

One of Ridgefield's most frightening mysteries occurred in 1982, when, in separate incidents, two young teenagers were accosted and stabbed in woods bordering the Mimosa subdivision off North Street. Fortunately, neither was seriously hurt.

A little before 9:00 p.m. on November 21, a few days before Thanksgiving, a fourteen-year-old boy went to the edge of woodland behind his house on Mimosa Circle to untangle a dog chain. Suddenly, he was "pulled into the woods and stabbed in the stomach," the *Ridgefield Press* reported. He was taken to the hospital and underwent exploratory surgery for the wound.

In its first statement on the incident, police did not specify that the boy was attacked. "As the victim entered the wooded area, he received a stab-type wound to the stomach," a press release said the next day. "Exactly how the wound was sustained is undetermined at this time." Detectives apparently wondered whether the wound was the result of a fall.

However, five days later, a girl, also fourteen years old, was walking in woods bordering Mimosa when she passed a man in his mid-twenties. The man then turned and "assaulted her with a sharp instrument," inflicting a minor cut to the right side of her abdomen.

Ridgefield Police captain Richard Bellagamba told reporters the department believed both stabbings were the work of one person—"someone who knows the area."

The girl described the assailant as "a white male in his mid-twenties, approximately 5 feet 10 inches tall, with medium-length brown hair." Using her facial descriptions, a composite drawing of a suspect was put together and distributed widely.

The initial uncertainty over how the boy's wound had occurred prompted many Mimosa neighbors to speculate that he may have simply fallen on something sharp or might even have been attacked by a deer. However, said a Mimosa resident at the time, the second stabbing made the boy's claim of being attacked "very, very believable."

The attacks prompted Mimosa residents as well as many in other neighborhoods along North Street to get involved in safety campaigns. Parents were told to maintain a closer watch over their children, lock their doors and keep outdoor lights shining in their yards. A Mimosa Homeowners Association letter to all residents advised, "Children should not go into the woods anywhere for the time being" and that "people should travel in pairs."

School Superintendent Elliott Landon recommended, temporarily at least, that children not walk each day to the nearby Scotland School (Barlow Mountain was closed then).

A Mimosa resident told the *Press* that neighbors felt the assailant appeared very familiar with the woods and was either someone who had lived in the area or someone who had spent a great deal of time there, such as a former resident or a friend of a resident.

For many weeks afterward, police flooded the area with patrols and investigated a number of leads. "There was much manpower expended on the case," current Police Chief John Roche recalled; he was a young patrolman at the time. However, in the end, no one was ever charged.

And no more stabbings occurred.

Chapter 3

BURNINGS AND THE DEVIL

In the 1970s, Satanic sects and a pair of firebugs brought the kind of flames that Ridgefield didn't want. And then there were the "book burnings."

SATANISM BENEATH A FULL MOON

Few episodes in Ridgefield's long history were more unusual or downright bizarre than the events of June 10, 1979. Early that Sunday morning, a Ridgefield policeman was accosted by four hooded men who were said to be singing in a strange tongue under a full moon on the grounds of a convent.

The headline in the *Ridgefield Press* distilled the story into eight words: "Hooded Chanters Attack Cop; Satanism Beneath Full Moon?"

The mysterious assault occurred around 2:30 a.m. and, according to *Press* reporters Burt Kearns and Larry Fossi, "may have involved a satanic cult, the likes of which has apparently existed in Ridgefield for four years."

The police officer was on a routine patrol that night when he heard strange sounds coming from woods off Oscaleta Road, land then owned by the Congregation of Notre Dame and now home of Ridgefield Academy.

The Quebec-based nuns had used the former estate as their motherhouse, headquarters for their operations in the United States.

According to the bare-bones police accounts at the time, the officer stopped his patrol car to listen more closely and heard voices chanting in unison in a strange language. He radioed the police station about his discovery and then began walking into the woods to investigate. He approached an unknown number of people wearing black hoods and was attacked by four of them.

The twenty-four-year-old patrolman seized one of the hooded attackers in a chokehold but was struck in the face by another, sources inside the police department told the *Press*. He then sprayed Mace at his attackers, retreated to his car and turned on its siren. The attackers fled.

The policeman radioed for help and was taken by ambulance to Danbury Hospital, where he was treated for head injuries, many cuts and bruises.

A police dog was brought in to try to trace the attackers but was unsuccessful. Police undertook what Chief Thomas Rotunda called a "full-scale investigation" of the incident.

Reporters Kearns and Fossi found that several residents in the Oscaleta Road area had been awakened early that Sunday morning by two explosions that "sounded like a gun going off, or a car backfiring."

Several of the people also heard music, which they described as "strange" and intermittently audible, from an area east of Oscaleta Road and north of Pumping Station Road.

Exploring the woods there, the reporters discovered a clearing in the trees with an unobstructed view of a large arc of the sky. Tall grass in the clearing had been recently trampled.

"Just past a tree wrapped with pieces of clothesline were large pieces of charred wood lying perpendicular to one another," they wrote. "The pieces of wood were placed too far from each other to have been used in a campfire, an observation supported by the absence of both embers and a cleared area around the wood. Several long poles were also found in a nearby area. The tips of the poles had been sharpened and burned."

A groundskeeper for the property said he had never burned anything there.

Charred and sharpened sticks were found near where a policeman was assaulted by hooded chanters. Ridgefield Press *photo by Larry Fossi, Ridgefield Historical Society archives.*

Cult activity had been suspected in Ridgefield before the run-in with the hooded chanters. A late March arrest of two Ridgefield men yielded a cache of knives, chains and black candles—all widely used accessories in satanic rituals.

The two reporters interviewed a nineteen-year-old Ridgefield youth who claimed to be a member of a cult called the Satanic Organization of Connecticut, allegedly involving about fifteen people ages seventeen to twenty in the Greater Danbury area but centered in Ridgefield. He said he didn't believe his cult's members were involved in the Sunday incident but said a full-moon ritual could have been the work of other cultists from Stamford or Danbury, part of a larger statewide satanic organization.

The youth said he wished to promote devil worship and to dispel misconceptions about it. "I've always liked witchcraft," he was quoted as saying. "I've read a lot about it. Ever since I was in sixth grade, I've read a lot about it."

He said the Ridgefield group met as often as three times a week in homes or parking lots. "We use the satanic bible—you can buy it in a bookstore for about $1.95. It explains the rituals." Members often smoked marijuana before or after the rituals but never during the ceremonies, he said.

"Rituals begin with readings from the satanic bible, and a recitation of the 72 infernal names—different names for the devil culled from Western literature," the reporters wrote. "Then candles of various colors are lit, and cultist waved knives or machetes in the air." They did not, the youth said, kill animals—or people.

The youth, a jobless high school dropout, said, "I go with the devil instead of God because the devil's been the underdog for 2,000 years. Hitler, Alexander the Great, Napoleon—they were all involved with the devil....

"Everybody will believe in Satan in about six or seven years," he added, with voice never wavering. "It is a fact."

Ridgefield police checked out all of the relatively few homes in the area of Oscaleta and Pumping Station Roads, even in the middle of the night. One woman reported her house was visited at three o'clock in the morning. According to Kearns and Fossi, "The officers, curious about the secluded house, shined flashlights in her window, then knocked on the door, asked to see her identification and proof that she lived there." The next day, she said, two police investigators came and expressed a particular interest in a strange, devil-like mask that hung above her fireplace. The mask had been made by a friend, the woman said, adding, "It looks like the devil, and they figured maybe I worshipped it."

Officers investigating the cultists' assault on a policeman were suspicious when they saw this mask. Ridgefield Press *photo by Larry Fossi, Ridgefield Historical Society archives.*

While one officer continued to interview her, another walked around the house, and then both toured the surrounding woods. "It was later learned that the police were considering a connection between the mask and the cop-beating," the reporters said.

The Reverend Edward Schultz, then assistant pastor of St. Stephen's Episcopal Church, had long been interested in the occult, as well as magic and extrasensory perception. Schultz, who preferred to be called "Father Edd," had spoken about Satanism and the occult two years earlier at a meeting of the Ridgefield Clergy Association. After the talk, two Ridgefield High School students—one a member of his parish—had come up to him.

"They said they were approached by some members of a cult or coven in town," Father Edd said. "They asked me if they should join. I told them no. They mentioned that it met somewhere near the high school, but they were a little unclear if it was a Satan worship or witchcraft."

Father Edd said, "High school students are especially vulnerable to the attractions of this kind of cult activity. High school kids feel like powerless people, and this gives them the feeling that they have some mysterious supernatural kind of power," especially through the psychological manipulation of others, both inside and outside the cult.

"Psychological damage can be done from Satan worship because the emphasis is on being out for yourself, and it doesn't matter what you do to anybody else."

Father Edd smiled and would not comment when asked if the police had spoken to him about the incident on Oscaleta Road. However, he confessed that he was tempted to call the *Press* after reading about the hoods worn by the attackers. In his extensive library, he said, he had several occult books that provided sewing patterns for making such hoods.

He warned of the dangers of high school Satanists. "This 'pee-wee league' involvement could lead to another, more serious involvement," he said. "People who are into it usually begin with small timers. It's sort of like drugs."

"Most people don't take it seriously," he added. "But they don't see the results of it. The cop was beaten. He could have been killed."

———

What began as "a game" resulted in serious involvement with illicit sex, hallucinogenic drugs and violence for a young Ridgefield woman who agreed to be interviewed by Fossi and Kearns in the presence of her mother.

The woman began her lengthy involvement with a devil-worshiping cult after a Ridgefield High School classmate introduced her to it. While it was Danbury-based, half the members came from Ridgefield, she said. Several were in their twenties, but many were high school students. The group performed satanic rituals in wooded areas of Ridgefield and Danbury, including a location off Oscaleta Road. Ceremonies involved using hoods, robes, candles and knives and often included drug use and sex.

"There was a lot of violence and animal sacrifices—goats, dogs and cats," she said. "At first, it was just a game for me. But after a while it was total. I would have stabbed my mother if somebody told me to. I didn't care."

The cultists, she said, were dangerous. "With what they're fooling around with, and what they're involved with, they don't care about anything. And they would do anything."

With the help of her family, the woman was eventually able to divorce herself from the Satanists, but she said it took several years to recover from the effects of her association with the cult.

———

A young man who claimed to be a lieutenant in the Satanic Organization of Connecticut maintained that his group held a much more benign view of Satanism and disapproved of illegal activities, including animal sacrifices, drug use and illicit sex. "Satanism is a religion, just like worshipping God," said the man, who claimed he led some ten thousand Satan worshippers in Connecticut.

The cultists involved in the Oscaleta Road incident were "bad eggs" who would not follow the tenets of the state organization, he claimed. "They use drugs—dealing as well as taking. And they don't care about other people's rights. These guys would do anything—they don't care; they're very sick people."

———

The assaulted police officer quit his job three months after the attack. In an interview, he said, "One of the reasons I am leaving is to further my education, although I am also leaving for personal reasons that at this time I am not at liberty to discuss because I feel obligated to the chief and the commission."

The union representing the rank and file officers claimed the policeman was "drummed out" because of "embarrassment" the incident caused the department. Union president Paul McAllister filed a handful of grievances, including a prohibitive practices action because the Police Commission had demanded that the officer return to the Connecticut Police Academy for ten weeks of retraining if he wanted to stay on the force. No officer in the history of the department—and perhaps the state—had been sent back to the academy, said McAllister, who claimed the move was aimed at embarrassing the officer. Because of the resignation, the prohibitive practice action was dropped.

Chief Rotunda denied that the resignation had anything to do with the Oscaleta Road attack and said that the retraining was part of an effort to help the police officer.

The Police Commission accepted the resignation "with regret." Anthony Chianese, a commission member, tried and failed to get his fellow members to discuss the officer's "personal reasons" for leaving and felt the commission had not handled the officer's case well.

"I feel badly that we were unable to do more" for the officer, he said.

No one was ever arrested in connection with the assault on the patrolman.

In a strange coincidence, five weeks later and one mile to the west of the site of the "satanic assault," a seventeen-year-old hired hand at the South Salem home of rock star Keith Richards and his common-law wife, Anita Pallenberg, shot himself in the head while lying in Pallenberg's bed and died two hours later. The Rolling Stones star was in Paris recording an album when the shooting occurred on July 20, 1979.

Pallenberg said she and the teenager had been watching television coverage of the tenth anniversary of man landing on the moon when the youth began playing Russian roulette with a .38-caliber pistol. She was cleared of any involvement in the death. Reports that the thirty-seven-year-old actress and model was having an affair with the boy in hopes that Richards, who had taken up with a different woman, would be jealous generated extensive tabloid media coverage.

The boy's death was eventually ruled a suicide. He had run away from his South Salem home several months after his mother, in excruciating pain from several ailments, had committed suicide.

His death, reports of wild parties at Richards's large eighteenth-century farmhouse and the proximity to the supposed Satanic ceremony a mile away in Ridgefield led some to wonder whether there was a connection between the South Salem shooting and the Ridgefield assault.

In discussing Pallenberg, Marlon Richards says in his father's autobiography, *Life*, "There were all these stories in the press at the time saying that she was a witch, that people were having Black Sabbaths. They were saying all sorts of things." No evidence was ever found that the Ridgefield event was connected with the nearby Richards homestead.

FIREBUGS ON THE LOOSE

"Officials Probe Seven Fires" announced the headline atop the front page of the December 5, 1974 *Ridgefield Press*. Four suspicious fires had taken place that week; three of them destroyed vacant structures, while a fourth damaged the fabric department of the W.T. Grant department store at Copps Hill Plaza. Also under investigation were two forest fires on November Sundays within one hundred yards of each other in Pierrepont State Park.

Police—and the public—feared an arsonist was at work. And, as it turned out, it was two arsonists.

On Monday, December 4, an old house deep in the woods of Peaceable Ridge Road was reported ablaze around 6:35 p.m. As soon as firefighters arrived there, the call from Grant's came in.

Then the next night, a blaze visible in three towns lit up the sky as a long-unused wooden water tower, owned by IBM, had been set afire off Great Hill Road. Again, as soon as the firemen reached the site, another alarm was sounded, this one for a burning house on Old West Mountain Road.

"What the hell's going on in this town?" one firefighter at the water tower exclaimed as the second alarm came over his portable two-way radio.

———

Suspicious fires since November 4 had destroyed a two-century-old house in Ridgebury, a small barn and a shack. Fire Marshal Francis P. Moylan met with police detectives to mull over the series of blazes, and detectives spent hours sifting through ashes and debris at the fire sites, taking pictures and interviewing neighbors. Moylan told reporters that he suspected arson in most, if not all, of the fires.

Two circumstances were common to six of the seven fires: they occurred after dark and involved structures that were not inhabited. At least four involved places known to have been frequented by teenagers for drinking, smoking or partying: the water tower, the Ridgebury house, a barn off High Ridge and the Old West Mountain Road house.

The last place, long empty and dilapidated, had been known in the neighborhood as "The Haunted House." Firefighters had considerable difficulty reaching the place, located at the end of a long, steep dirt road. Mud up to six inches deep made the incline almost impossible to negotiate, and it took firemen more than twenty minutes to get a truck up the path.

Meanwhile, firefighters diverted to Grant's found employees had extinguished the fire. Grant's officials felt a carelessly dropped cigarette caused the fire, but a police source said no evidence of a cigarette was found, and the condition of the burned material seemed to suggest that it was ignited by something other than a cigarette.

The water tower fire, 750 feet above sea level in the Great Hill Road woods, was perhaps the most spectacular. The structure, built around 1915 and designed to hold ninety thousand gallons, was 40 feet high and made mostly of huge timbers. The tower had supplied water and pressure to the old Outpost Farm estate of Colonel Louis D. Conley, and because it had not been used in decades, the wood was tinder dry. What's more, high winds were feeding the blaze and sending thousands of glowing embers across the woodland. Fortunately, the ground was damp from recent rains. The existence of the tower, in deep woods, was not widely known, except to teenagers who partied there. (About a year earlier, detectives had uncovered a portion of the loot from a burglary stashed near the tower.)

A dilapidated 1755 house on Ridgebury Road, opposite the entrance to the golf course, burned early on the morning of November 4. Ironically, good eventually came from evil; the foundation and chimney of this arson victim became the basis for the rectory of the new St. Elizabeth Seton Church complex on the property, purchased a couple years after the fire.

On the evening of November 4, a barn on High Ridge and Bryon Avenues burned down. The Pierrepont Park fires occurred on November 10 and 24.

The *Press* also learned that several days before Thanksgiving, an attempt was made to set fire to the Little League field house at Aldrich Park.

Not only the fire and police departments but also the whole town was growing apprehensive about the mysterious fires. But the break came less than a week later.

Detectives had been patrolling areas near several buildings considered prospects for arson. On Thursday, December 5, they stopped a car on Copps Hill Road containing two teenagers, ages eighteen and nineteen. Shining a flashlight through a window into the back seat, the detectives noticed a five-gallon plastic can of gasoline.

The two were brought to police headquarters, where, after hours of questioning, the eighteen-year-old confessed that the pair had burned down six buildings—but did not ignite the Grant's fire.

What's more, when they were pulled over, they were on their way to set fire to the former state police barracks on East Ridge—a building slated to become the new Ridgefield Police headquarters.

The two were charged with a total of eighty-two felonies and misdemeanors, including six counts each of arson and conspiracy to commit arson, as well as various counts of burglary, criminal mischief (vandalism) and criminal trespassing. And just for good measure, the police added six counts of "reckless burning."

The teenagers failed to post $10,000 bond and were held in the Bridgeport jail. They were eventually convicted and did time in prison.

Both arsonists wound up dying young. The nineteen-year-old was killed five years later when his speeding car went out of control on Route 7 in nearby Danbury and slammed into a tree. The eighteen-year-old died in 1990 at the age of thirty-four of an undisclosed cause; he was by then married with children.

THE DOG IN A TREE

It started with sex, peaked with the hanging of a dog and wound up as national news. The so-called book-burnings of the early 1970s had gotten so bad that reporters, including a Pulitzer Prize winner, descended on Ridgefield to try to figure out just what was going on.

Leo Carroll reads from *Soul on Ice* before seven hundred people at a school board hearing in February 1972. Ridgefield Press *photo by the author, Ridgefield Press archives.*

The battle over books used in the schools began around 1970. By then, the town's population had reached just over eighteen thousand, more than doubling in a decade, and therein lay some of the problem. The town's rapid growth and attractiveness to large families brought many new children to town. More children meant more schools, and more schools brought more taxes needed to build and operate them. Old-timers and those with modest incomes were feeling the pinch as taxes rose much faster than the normal rate of inflation of 5 to 10 percent a year.

Consequently, some voters who had for years supported sophisticated school programs began scrutinizing government budgets, particularly education spending—the biggest consumer of tax dollars. That sparked wars in the 1960s and '70s between many parents, who wanted a top-notch education for their children, and taxing conservatives, who wanted the schools to offer a basic education, without the "frills," as they often called them.

Adding to the turmoil was the closing of St. Mary's School in June 1970 after lack of vocations led the teaching nuns to depart. Many parents who'd hoped their children would have a parochial education were now forced to use the public schools. Thus, the content of the public school curriculum began to figure into efforts to reshape the schools. And the first battle of the decade erupted over sex education.

Concerned Parents will not accept any program in which students are brought together in groups large or small for the purpose of discussing under anyone's leadership (adult or student) the problems of sex, dating, growing up, peer group acceptance, being loved and cared for, home and school pressures, smoking, drinking and health.

That was part of a statement from a group called Concerned Parents of Ridgefield, reacting in April 1970 to the Board of Education's plans to begin a federally funded program at the East Ridge Junior High School. Project TELL, as the program was called, was aimed at providing sex education and other forms of modern health instruction. "We consider any such activity as part of the school's curriculum or programs an unacceptable and unjustifiable incursion on the right of privacy of both children and their parents," said Norman Little, an airline pilot and a father of seven, who was the head of Concerned Parents.

The group focused especially on sex education and, in May, presented ten speakers and a thirty-minute sound film strip called *Sex Education: Conditioning for Immorality*. The film was produced by a California company that the Anti-Defamation League called "a far-right propaganda operation" operated by a former leader of the John Birch Society. Parents accused the schools of creating programs for "indoctrinating students in sex attitudes," the *Ridgefield Press* reported. One mother observed, "Modern citizens suffer from a lack of formation, not information."

In September, the group began also attacking a book, *Playing It Cool*, which was being used in junior high English classes. Norman Little maintained it was full of themes like hate, despair and doubt that were "whittling away all those things which we consider good in this country."

By October, the Board of Education had heard enough criticism and voted 6–0 to drop Project TELL.

Around the same time, another group called the Ridgefield Taxpayers League was gaining strength and began attacking the school board on several fronts, not the least of which was a new rule in which the board limited public comment at meetings to five minutes. "The taxpayers refuse to be muzzled," said league president Louis A. Garofalo, calling the limit a "gag rule" and telling the board it would be ignored.

"Are you threatening us?" school board chairman Robert S. Haight asked him.

"That's not a threat, it's a promise," shouted Garofalo. (Two years later, police were called to evict Garofalo and others from a school board meeting.)

Critics, including Garofalo, started demanding a list of all paperback books used in the school system. Some paperbacks, said Arlene Sharp of Concerned Parents, are contributing to "the moral bankruptcy in the schools." Teachers were also criticized for voicing "any opinion they want in class."

In the late fall of 1970, under constant pressure from critics over some of the books used in the schools, the Board of Education adopted a new policy on the selection of textbooks and the hearing of complaints about them—a policy teachers viewed as infringing on academic freedom. Some books, like *Playing It Cool*, were dropped from the curriculum. Among the books that Concerned Parents also wanted removed were titles that included the writings of people like Thomas Jefferson, Dwight Eisenhower, Alexander Hamilton, George Wallace and Malcolm X.

In December, confrontations between the critics and officials grew more intense. A worried Ridgefield Teachers Association issued a statement deploring the criticisms of staff and curriculum. "It is time to speak out clearly and forcefully against these attacks," the teachers said, asking to meet with the school board.

A January 21 conference between the school board and teachers, scheduled for private session, was cancelled after more than forty people threatened a sit-in. "If you go into executive session, I'm going to sit down on my chair and I'm not going to budge," said John Longden, a member of the Ridgefield Taxpayers League.

"I couldn't believe that this was Ridgefield," said a teacher who reported that several fellow teachers were followed and heckled after the cancelled meeting. "The teachers were called 'pinko,' 'communist,' 'bums,' and one teacher had 'the legitimacy of her birth questioned,'" the teacher told the *Press*. "It was a horrifying experience."

Things got worse. A full-page ad in the *Press*, sponsored by several groups including Concerned Parents and the Taxpayers League, maintained that "the basic issue is not book-burning, but garbage removal. It is our position that the schools are wasting the students' time and taxpayers' money."

Many parents, upset at the removal of textbooks from courses, met with the chairmen of the English and social studies departments of the secondary schools to figure out how to convince the school board to change its mind about the banned books. They wound up at least partially successful, and in March 1971, the board voted to reinstate *Hamilton vs. Jefferson*; *Voices of Dissent*; and *Police, Courts and the Ghetto*, all used in the eighth grade.

The fighting seemed to die down for a while, but the following year brought new confrontations, leading to a widely publicized period of the book-banning battle. This time, the target was a bestseller, *Boss: Richard Daley of Chicago*, used as supplemental reading in a high school senior year class on contemporary American politics. Under its new policy, the board was voting on all books used in the schools, and Chairman Lodi Kysor cast a tie-breaking vote against using *Boss*. "I don't think it's a good book," she said. "I don't think it's a well-written book. Therefore I'm going to vote against it."

Board member A. Raymond Bessette considered it "trash," and member Samuel DiMuzio said, "I don't think this is the kind of book to spend our money on.…It's a totally negative book." Joseph Negreen, a parent critic, said, "I believe it's all part of the giant conspiracy in this country by such well-placed characters" as the president of the teachers association and the chairman of the social studies department.

The book's author was Mike Royko, a popular Chicago newspaper columnist. When Royko heard about the ban, he called the Ridgefield school

Nationally syndicated cartoonist Jerry Marcus, who lived in Ridgefield, drew this editorial cartoon for the *Ridgefield Press* during the "book-burning" crisis. Ridgefield Press *archives.*

board a bunch of "rubes." That same year, Royko won the Pulitzer Prize for commentary—not about Ridgefield, however.

The ban sparked an explosion of reaction among many Ridgefielders. The *Press* had so many letters that it devoted a special section to them on April 20; petitions signed by 1,000 of the 1,075 students at the high school demanded the book's reinstatement; and free copies of *Boss* were being offered to high school juniors and seniors by Books Plus, a local bookstore.

Under tremendous pressure, the school board gathered again and reversed its vote, allowing *Boss* as supplemental reading.

But Bessette, who was among those who changed his vote, was angry. He said he had resigned as president of the Ridgefield Athletic Association Corporation (RAAC), an organization through which he had almost single-handedly built the town's new ice skating center. "The hate letters and abusive phone calls have intimidated neither my family nor myself," he said. "But realizing the viciousness of the backlash could affect completely unrelated projects," he said, he felt he had to resign his RAAC leadership.

The book controversy continued through 1972, with Concerned Parents attacking new titles, but the most heated episode occurred in early January 1973, when one of the school board's own members—the venerable Leo F. Carroll—announced that he wanted two books, *Soul on Ice* by Eldridge Cleaver and *Police, Courts and the Ghetto*, subject of a past battle, removed from the schools.

Some were surprised that the usually open-minded Carroll would propose the banning of two books—one of which had already gone through considerable debate two years earlier. And even Carroll himself, as he would later admit to a reporter, was taken aback by the uproar he would cause.

Carroll had spent many years as a state policeman, rising through the ranks to become second in command of the entire state police force. After a stint on the Liquor Control Commission, he served for ten years as a popular first selectman, or chief executive, of Ridgefield, retiring in 1967. But he had spent his life in state and local government, and his retirement from town hall left him looking for a new form of public service. When a vacancy occurred on the school board in 1969, he became a candidate and easily won the seat.

Both books offended Carroll, chiefly because they were severely critical of police—a profession in which he had spent much of his life. But Carroll was also a bit "old school" and could not condone, for student consumption, the "terrible worlds" and "bad words" found in Cleaver's book. "Why he even takes a crack at our President and refers to him as Dirty Dick," Carroll said at a public hearing, prompting much laughter, even applause, among the seven hundred people in the audience. (The nation was in the midst of the Watergate scandal.)

At the same hearing, he read a passage in which Cleaver said, "I became a rapist. To refine my technique and modus operandi, I started practicing on black girls in the ghetto.…When I considered myself smooth enough, I crossed the tracks and sought white prey."

Another school board member told the crowd that the excerpt was taken out of context. Stanley Gianzero pointed out that Cleaver then wrote, "I took a long look at myself and, for the first time in my life, admitted that I was wrong, that I had gone astray…for I could not approve the act of rape."

The *Soul on Ice* debate quickly sparked a lot of bitterness, but the most shocking example occurred in mid-January. Elfrieda Travostino, the head of the Ridgefield Teachers Association, announced that the staff was "fed up" over the book issue and other educational problems and that unless the teachers and school board could quickly work out a way to improve the climate in the schools, teachers would go on a one-day protest strike on January 29.

A few days after her announcement, Travostino was in her Ridgefield home when the phone rang. She went to the living room to answer it and noticed her front door open and her large poodle missing. "We have muzzled your dog," the phone caller said. "If you don't shut your loud mouth, your kids and you will be next."

Travostino told police she rushed outside and found her sixty-pound poodle hanging by its choke collar from the trunk of a tree. The dog had managed to keep one foot on the ground and was not seriously injured, Travostino told the *Press*.

Around the same time, Attorney William Laviano announced the formation of an American Civil Liberties committee in Ridgefield "to deal with book issues and other civil rights questions involving the town," the *Press* said. Almost immediately, he said, he was receiving threatening phone calls.

Police investigated both cases but never found a suspect.

The brouhaha quickly attracted national attention. Film crews became a common sight at school board meetings as local and national TV began covering the "book-burning" in Ridgefield.

Among the many journalists who descended on the town was Jack Nelson, then a reporter for the *Los Angeles Times*. Nelson, winner of a Pulitzer Prize in journalism, had a particular interest in the subject; he was coauthor of the 1963 book *The Censors and the Schools*, which exposed many forms of book censorship in school systems across the country and even in publishing houses. Nelson spent several days in town and wound up writing

Pulitzer Prize–winning journalist Jack Nelson came to Ridgefield to cover the book controversy. *Jack Nelson Tributes blog.*

several pieces, including a two-thousand-word story that was published by newspapers in many states.

Book-banning battles "have flared off and on across the country for decades, usually initiated by conservative or anti-obscenity groups that fear students will be corrupted by books that do not adhere to the groups' standard of patriotism or decency," he wrote. "In recent years, new school courses on ethnic studies and books focusing on ghetto life and other race-related problems, including unequal administration of justice, have sparked an increasing number of attacks on books."

After many meetings, most involving large audiences, the school board in early February decided with a 5–4 vote to leave the books in the curriculum for the rest of the year but then to review whether to retain the courses they were used in. That didn't sit well with many, including students who turned in petitions signed by one thousand students opposing any removal of books or courses. A *Danbury News-Times* poll found that 67 percent of the townspeople agreed with the decision to leave *Soul on Ice* in the schools.

As if the school board did not have enough problems, it voted the following month to fire the school superintendent, Dr. David E. Weingast, himself the author of four books of American history. According to Weingast, his contract was terminated because "responsible officials suggested that I take certain actions affecting some members of the staff. The proposals, I felt, were punitive and improper, and I rejected them." He would give no more detail, but the assumption was the "certain actions" were connected with the book-banning battles.

In a matter probably unrelated to his firing, Dr. Weingast received on May 4, 1973, a letter of resignation from Paul Nimchek, a popular math teacher at Ridgefield High School, who took a job in nearby New Fairfield. "The circumstances in the school system during the past year have had, in my opinion, a detrimental effect on the educational system in Ridgefield," he explained. "Therefore, I personally find it necessary to seek a new educational atmosphere in which to teach."

The year before, the Ridgefield Jaycees had named Nimchek "Outstanding Young Educator" of 1972. As a math teacher, he was not even a likely target of book critics.

The school system turmoil prompted the Ridgefield Teachers Association to ask the Connecticut Education Association "to inquire into the freedom to teach in Ridgefield," said Paul Fako, teacher president. By then, a shaken Travostino had resigned and Fako had taken over.

In the end, *Soul on Ice* remained on the reading list for a senior ethnic studies course, but *Police, Courts and the Ghetto* was dropped as part of a major overhaul of the eighth-grade social studies curriculum. The action was approved on a 6–2 vote in May, with Carroll one of the two opposing.

The school board also backed down on the termination of Weingast's contract, and he remained superintendent until he reached the retirement age of sixty-five in 1977. Asked then if he might be interested in running for a seat on the school board that had provided so much trouble for him over the years, he replied, "Never! I couldn't be dragooned or seduced or bought!"

In October 1973, the Connecticut Education Association published a thirty-eight-page booklet called *Responsible Academic Freedom: Challenge to Ridgefield*, which criticized "academic vandalism" in Ridgefield. The six-member investigative team found that "a climate of public attack against teachers and teaching methods has been allowed to develop in Ridgefield to such an extent that a pall has been cast over the entire educational system." It maintained that the critics were "relatively few in number, but persistent and vociferous in pressing their charges. Defenders and supporters of teachers and programs are greater in number but less persistent, vociferous and organized." It found the school board "at critical junctures failed to follow and to insist on constituents following established policies and procedures, and thus has helped to bring about public disarray and destructive diversion in the schools." Teachers themselves weren't without blame, it added; they "on occasion appear to have overreacted to attacks and to have thus had the effect of adding fuel to the fires."

Attacks on books and curriculum soon dwindled and all but disappeared. Relations between the school board and staff—and the community— improved as new members were elected to the board.

Then, a couple of years of calm later, during the public comments portion of a school board meeting, a parent stood up and questioned the use of a book in the schools.

Many members of the board looked aghast. Some rolled their eyes. The board thanked the speaker, moved on to the agenda and never brought up the subject again.

Chapter 4

PROBLEMS WITH PREJUDICE

R acial and ethnic biases have led to some ugly behavior in Ridgefield's past.

THE IMMIGRANT ITALIANS

The late nineteenth-century influx of immigrants from Europe, especially Italy, sparked suspicion among the staid old New England farmers of Ridgefield, unaccustomed to the strange languages and odd accents being spoken in their town. But neither the Germans nor the Irish, who began coming to Ridgefield in the mid-1800s, suffered as much as the Italians—the underdogs of yesterday who now are among the leaders of the town.

The Italian community in the late nineteenth and early twentieth centuries consisted of many people who could speak little or no English, often lived in what would today be considered slums, dressed differently and mostly did manual labor. Newspaper accounts of immigrants strongly reflected a sense that they were looked down upon. It was not unusual to see a news story that said simply "an Italian" was involved in some incident, never even bothering with a name—which, more often than not, was misspelled when it did appear. The Italian newcomers were considered foreigners. When an old building housing workers on a state road construction project in town burned down in 1920, the *Ridgefield Press* headline said: "Fatal Fire at Branchville; Former Seth Beers Store, Used to House State Road Gang, Totally Consumed—All Italian Occupants Escape—Only American in Gang Dies in Flames."

The Italians began moving here in the late 1880s, mostly to work on estates and construction projects like the new sewer and water lines and roads for the Port of Missing Men resort on West Mountain. And it was estate workers who figured in an 1893 incident that, in a couple of ways, reflected the low esteem in which Italian immigrants were held at the time. And yet, it also suggested that not everyone was bigoted.

A MURDEROUS SHOT

In a lengthy front-page story headlined "A Murderous Shot," the newspaper chronicled the incident involving Jerry Crystonan, a laborer working on the huge estate of Henry deBevoise Schenck on Florida Hill Road called Downesbury Manor.

At around 6:00 p.m. on a Sunday in late August, Crystonan was walking to the village, accompanied by Frank Caspera, a fourteen-year-old lad who had frequently offered shoe-shining services on Main Street. Without much journalistic neutrality, the *Press* described Crystonan as "nearly six feet tall,

Both Jerry Crystonan and the fourteen-year-old boy he shot lived on the Downesbury Manor estate on Florida Hill Road. *Ridgefield Historical Society archives.*

with heavy dark moustache, and flat fierce-looking face, peculiarly scarred on the chin, his countenance presenting sharply the Italian underhand cunning that will stab in the dark."

As they were approaching the village, Crystonan told the boy to stop following him and to return to what the newspaper called "the Italian shanty" on the Schenck estate. Caspera refused and continued to follow Crystonan, who then slapped the boy across the face and again told him to scram.

"The lad seemed determined to follow his brutal companion when the latter, without warning, drew a revolver and fired the bullet, piercing the abdominal parts," the *Press* said. "The would-be murderer fled precipitately."

Several people heard the shot and rushed to the scene. The boy was taken to a nearby house and three doctors were summoned; two responded. "It was found by the physicians that the bullet, probably shot from a .22 caliber revolver, had entered the abdomen in front and finally lodged in the loins," the newspaper reported. "Probing was considered dangerous. The physicians rendered such medical and surgical aid as was possible but felt convinced the wound would prove fatal."

The fact that so much help responded was a sign that there were kind and caring people in Ridgefield. However, at the same time physicians were being summoned, so was Thomas C. White, the deputy sheriff of Ridgefield. Unlike the doctors, however, White declined to respond and declared he would look into the case in the morning. The fact that an Italian man had shot an Italian boy did not seem important enough. The next morning, he and Constable Willis Powers did begin their investigation.

The *Press* editor was furious, writing:

> Because of the delay of several hours in getting the legal wheels in motion, Sheriff White has been generally censured by all believers in law and order who know the circumstances of the case. It is said quite authoritatively that after the shooting, the would-be murderer went directly to the Italian quarters and remained there till after 2 o'clock the next morning, thus giving an officer of the law abundant opportunity to make an arrest, had he not been too tired and sleepy. Perhaps the deputy sheriff had good and sufficient reasons for not acting immediately, but few people here are convinced that he did his whole duty as an officer sworn to protect life and ferret the criminal. It is said that several able-bodied men awaited the arrival of the sheriff, in readiness to aid the officer in finding and arresting the criminal, and they are justly indignant because the man was allowed to escape.

Indeed, Crystonan did escape and was never seen again in town. In his investigation of the shooting, the sheriff alleged that Crystonan was "a member of the dreaded Mafia and had sworn vengeance against the uncle of the boy he shot, because the uncle had testified against him, that testimony sending him to prison for several years." How reliable that finding was seems questionable.

Meanwhile, much to the surprise of the physicians and everyone else, the boy recovered from his seemingly mortal wound.

THE WAR PATH

When Italian names were used, they were often misspelled. A blatant example was several stories about a 1920 incident involving Italians and non-Italians that led to a local constable's shooting an Italian man whose name was spelled four different ways, and probably never correctly.

What's worse was how the local newspaper headlined the story in its October 12 edition: "Italians on War Path: Smash Windows, One Shot Escaping Officer."

On Thursday night, October 8, at around eight o'clock, "two local youths" were hanging out near the railroad depot on Prospect Street (now Ridgefield Supply Company). Clearly, the two were not of Italian ancestry, for the account reported, "One of them had an altercation with some Italians. It is alleged the Italians had used improper language to the companion of the youth. It also appears that one of the youths had previously had trouble with the Italians and that the latter held animosity toward him."

A "fracas" ensued in which "one of the youths knocked down an Italian" and then escaped by running behind the old Barhite building—now Gallo Restaurant—which was used as apartments. Apparently under the impression that the youth had sought refuge in the Barhite building, "and determined to wreak their revenge, the Italians broke out the door to the tenement quarters with a club and also smashed all the window lights by bombarding the building with cobblestones."

Needless to say, the people inside were terrified. "The inmates, not knowing the cause of the onslaught, were panic stricken when large stones came sailing through the windows." The rocks were big enough that, according to a later story, "any one…would have caused serious injury or death had it struck any of the inmates of the building."

The occupants ran from the house, and Constable Roswell L. Dingee was summoned.

Early Friday morning, Dingee went to Branchville and located one of the rowdies, John Giacomini—that's our guess as to the "correct" spelling of his name since several members of that family lived here; *Press* accounts had Gacimeni, Gacameni, Gacimme and Gacimmie.

As Dingee took the young man into custody, one of Giacomini's friends tackled the officer. "In the struggle, both got away," the *Press* reported. "The constable called upon his prisoner to halt. As the fleeing man paid no attention to the command, Constable Dingee fired and wounded the fugitive in the leg." Even wounded, Giacomini managed to escape.

It was probably the first time a Ridgefield police officer ever shot someone, although the story never said that.

The next issue of the *Press* reported that Dingee had learned his suspect fled to New Haven, and he got New Haven police to arrest Giacomini. Assisted by a private citizen, Dingee went to New Haven and took Giacomini into custody, charging him with assault, "breaking windows by throwing stones" and resisting an officer.

Back in Ridgefield, Justice Samuel Nicholas released Giacomini on a $500 bond, which was supplied by Tony Mai, a well-known and well-respected Ridgefielder who operated a trucking business.

The trial took place on Saturday, November 13, before Justice Nicholas in town hall. Giacomini pleaded guilty. Nicholas imposed a suspended jail sentence of thirty days and made him pay the costs of the case, amounting to forty-seven dollars.

Considering the sensational aspects of the case, including the shooting and the assault on an officer, this seemed an exceedingly mild sentence. One wonders whether there was testimony brought out that the Italian boys had been taunted into their misadventures by the townies, sparking the initial fight and the attack on the Barhite tenement. Or that Dingee had somehow mishandled the case—especially when he fired a gun at a suspect wanted for what was basically vandalism. Four years later, Justice Nicholas would severely chastise Dingee for his handling of a case in which Dingee arrested a man for drunken driving, even though he did not see the man drive—probably because Dingee himself was drunk at the time (see page 99).

The Giacomini case was prosecuted by Grand Juror Harry E. Hull, a young house painter and a veteran of World War I, who went on to become a well-liked and respected first selectman of the town in the 1940s and

1950s. He was also grand marshal of the Memorial Day Parade for more than a half century.

As for Giacomini, he is believed to have become a New Haven contractor specializing in building sidewalks and by 1940 was the proprietor of his own tavern in New Haven.

While the Italian community suffered poverty and bigotry for decades, Italian Americans not only endured but rose above both to become leaders in Ridgefield. Two first selectmen—Louis J. Fossi (1973–81) and Rudy Marconi (1999–present)—came from families of the early Italian immigrants. Paul and John Morganti, born in a Bailey Avenue tenement, became heads of a construction firm founded by their father, John, that built hundreds of schools, hospitals and other large buildings along the entire East Coast. Silvio Bedini, whose dad was an estate worker, became a curator at the Smithsonian Institution and the author of more than twenty books of history. Countless others—like Selectman Julius Tulipani, business owner and school board member Enzo Bartolucci, Public Works superintendent Frank Serfilippi, local radio and TV personality Paul Baker (née Baldaserini), local historian Aldo Biagiotti and Police Chief Richard Ligi—have been among the many leading Italian American citizens of Ridgefield.

The Beating of a Black Man

Blacks also suffered at the hands of local bigots. One of the most blatant cases of racism to appear in the pages of the *Press* occurred on September 30, 1922, and led to cries of injustice and to some embarrassing publicity for the local state police.

That evening, Robert Cooper had just finished eating at Coleman's Lunch, a small diner behind the town hall, and was chatting with James "Gus" Venus, the counterman. Cooper was a black chauffeur for a woman who had homes in North Salem and New York City and was a frequent visitor to Ridgefield. "He bears an excellent reputation as a peaceful, inoffensive person," the *Press* said.

Coleman's Lunch is shown behind town hall. The assault on Robert Cooper continued to Main Street, where the straw-hatted man stands. *Circa 1920 postcard in author's collection.*

Thomas Kelly came into the restaurant, saw Cooper and immediately ordered him to leave, "saying he would not eat with niggers," the *Press* reported. Cooper apparently ignored the demand, and Kelly "then struck the colored man a severe blow in the face and followed him out to Main Street, and struck and knocked him down and kicked him."

Bystanders rescued Cooper and brought him to Charles Riedinger's electrical shop on Bailey Avenue. "Kelly followed and with difficulty was restrained from renewing the assault," the newspaper said. Cooper "bled profusely" and was taken to Dr. B.A. Bryon's office on Main Street (where the CVS shopping center is today). "He was severely injured and is very likely to lose the sight of one eye," the *Press* account said.

One of the witnesses to the attack was seven-year-old Richard E. Venus, who was at Coleman's Lunch getting a hamburger from his older brother, Gus, the counterman. Dick Venus grew up to become Ridgefield's postmaster, a selectman and its first town historian.

Venus also wrote 366 historical columns in the *Press*, and in one in 1983 describing Coleman's diner, he said:

The little lunch wagon was the scene of so many happy and pleasant memories that it is sad to report that it was here that I witnessed the only act of racial prejudice that I have ever encountered in Ridgefield. A white man, from a well-known Ridgefield family, had apparently imbibed too much alcohol and refused to sit at the counter with a black man who was passing through town.

The white man was both verbally and physically abusive. The whole affair was quite sickening. Finally the State Police were called and he was placed under arrest. It made an impression that I will never forget.

The "well-known Ridgefield family" included Sergeant John C. Kelly, commander of the local state police barracks and brother of Thomas Kelly.

———

David W. Workman, the editor of the *Press*, was irate over the incident. The *Press* offices were in the Masonic Hall building, just south of town hall and spitting distance from Coleman's Lunch; it's possible someone on the staff witnessed at least some of the incident.

"AN INVESTIGATION NEEDED," said the bold, front-page headline over an account of the assault that was as much an editorial as it was a news story. Workman's article pointed out several disturbing facts.

"Roswell Dingee, a constable, was present at the time of the assault or immediately after, but made no attempt to arrest Kelly," Workman wrote. This is the same constable who had been involved in other controversial incidents such as arresting a man for drunk driving when he himself was drunk.

Thomas Kelly had disappeared for a few days. When he returned, state police arrested him for assault and breach of the peace and brought him before Justice Samuel Nicholas in the town court. "On the statement of the state policeman, a nominal fine was imposed on Kelly," the *Press* said. That fine was fifteen dollars plus court costs.

"Neither Michael Coleman nor the doctor nor any of the witnesses were subpoenaed or called to testify as to the nature of the assault or the severity of the injuries to the colored man," Workman wrote. "The justice had only the statement of the State Police to guide him in imposing punishment."

Editor Workman minced no words. "A brutal bully makes a most atrocious attack on an inoffensive peaceful man of good reputation, simply because he is a colored man, and he goes unpunished in this town," he wrote. "The state police take charge of the arrest and punishment of the bully and do not call Mr. Coleman or the doctor or any of the witnesses to testify to the assault or the seriousness of the crime so that the justice may know what punishment to inflict."

Workman then pointed out that "Thomas Kelly is a brother of John C. Kelly, head of the State Police in this town. Are relatives of the State Police exempt from punishment for crimes? Apparently an investigation should be made by those who appoint and control the State Police."

The fallout from the incident produced both positive and, apparently, negative results. On the negative side, the store of Charles Riedinger was broken into a few days later and, according to one account, "some goods taken, and other goods damaged so as to destroy their value."

An anonymous Ridgefielder who saw the burglary and vandalism as "vindictiveness" for Riedinger's helping out the injured black man sent the merchant a check for $100 (equal to around $1,400 today). "Every man and woman in Ridgefield must admit some responsibility for the town conditions," the donor said. "I thus feel that we should bear some share of your loss." The donor asked the Riedingers to accept the $100 "not as a gift, but as a share of your loss. I hope steps will be taken to bring those who are responsible for the Town Government, whether holding office or not, to some realization of the damage done to the standing, and therefore, the prosperity of the town."

At the same time, the *Press* continued its criticism of the state police, saying, "It is unfortunate that those guilty of the crime above mentioned have not been found and punished. We hear that the State Police neglected to take any fingerprints. This would seem gross neglect. We hope it is not true."

Meanwhile, the *Press*'s October 17 call for an investigation was having results. By December, eighteen Ridgefield women, upset at the apparent mishandling of the Cooper case, had petitioned Connecticut governor Everett J. Lake, demanding an investigation. "We make no criticisms of the present head of the [State Police] Department situated in Ridgefield, but we feel that it is imperative that we should have in this position [the investigator], an outsider, a man with no local affiliations, and of an age to command respect from his authority. We respectfully request that some higher official be delegated to come here and make an investigation."

Governor Lake thanked "the good women of Ridgefield" and immediately passed the buck to Robert T. Hurley, the superintendent—equivalent of chief—of the Connecticut State Police. Hurley wrote the petitioners, saying, "The complaint will be fully investigated." He asked to meet with them "and any other citizens who may be able to throw light on the matter."

The petitioners were not pleased with the response. They hired Attorney William Jerome.

William Travers Jerome (1858–1934) was no ordinary lawyer. Based in New York City, he had been a prominent district attorney in the city and "a man of

William Travers Jerome, a top New York City attorney, represented the Ridgefielders concerned about the beating of a black man. *Wikimedia Commons.*

wide experience and of the highest reputation in his profession," his clients said.

Indeed, District Attorney Jerome was famous for heading campaigns against political corruption and mob bosses, even personally leading raids on the criminals. In his most famous case, he prosecuted millionaire Harry Kendall Thaw for the murder of the noted architect Stanford White, who had been having an affair with Thaw's chorus girl wife. (Thaw was found not guilty by reason of insanity and sent to an asylum.)

Jerome's first cousin was Jennie Jerome, who became the wife of Sir Winston Churchill, the British prime minister.

Jerome told Superintendent Hurley he was hired because of "an apparently gross miscarriage of justice and grave dereliction of public duty in connection with the brutal assault committed in Ridgefield, by one Thomas Kelly, upon an inoffensive colored man."

He objected to Hurley's reply that he would meet with the women about the facts in the case, saying they clearly had no personal knowledge of the facts and that the reason they petitioned was to have someone in high authority determine those facts. "It seems to them that your request for a conference at the town hall was merely camouflage," he wrote. "They fancy that such a conference was designed only to humiliate them and to avoid making a real investigation which it seems to them it is your duty to make and for doing your duty the taxpayers pay you. Some are unkind enough to refer to an old saying that 'you don't hunt ducks with a brass band,' and to intimate that the best way to collect evidence of criminal acts is not by meetings and discussions with the police authorities in the town hall."

Jerome added, "Let me submit, that however unfair my clients may seem to you in these thoughts, the charge is a grave one and involves a serious dereliction of duty unless it be exhaustively investigated."

Hurley was not pleased either. "My first impulse on reading the more unreasonable portions of your letter was to make a categorical denial of all the principal facts," he wrote to Jerome in late December. "The department, however, prides itself on its unquestioned reputation and welcomes all fair-minded criticism. I am ready to take for granted the good faith of your clients, whatever their feelings towards me in this connection may be, and I feel sure that once I have clearly before me just what it is that these good people take issue with, that I can remove the misunderstanding."

"I personally have been satisfied as to the facts alluded to in the editorial," he said, without comment on whether he found the "facts" correct.

Hurley told Jerome that he had met with "many Ridgefield citizens" interested in the case, but none were apparently petitioners. He again asked that the eighteen identify themselves.

In March, Jerome noted that he was aware the department has sent "special representatives" to Ridgefield and felt that by now they should have been able to "fully ascertain the facts in this case."

He was now representing sixteen of the female signers to the petition to the governor, as well as "two men who are large taxpayers of Ridgefield and who also are officers of the Ridgefield Protective Society." The society, he said, consisted of "a large number of other owners of property at Ridgefield." They'd even hired a detective agency to look into the case, "at considerable expense."

He continued:

> As chief of a police organization, you are, or should be familiar with the criminal law of Connecticut and should know that a case of assault such as that which resulted in the petition which the governor referred to you, calls for a decision that would recognize the crime more nearly as a felony than as simply disorderly conduct. The trial at Ridgefield, however, resulted in only a fine of $15 and costs being imposed on the party charged with the crime. The lightness of this penalty as compared with the facts shown above in affidavits readily secured by a competent detective agency (and equally available to your men) suggests that in prosecuting this case, the local representatives of the state police at Ridgefield neglected to properly collect the evidence and adequately present it at trial. Whether this was due to incompetence, or intention in order to protect someone having political or other influence, it justifies anxiety on the part of Ridgefield residents as in whether they can count upon competent and impartial protection against crime.

The April 3, 1923 *Press* contains the last mention of the case, and no other records of what finally happened have been found. Hurley clearly investigated the charges that the case was mishandled, and if he found any fault, he may have dealt with it internally. However, it appears that Sergeant John Kelly was not blamed, for he continued to lead the local barracks and eventually rose through the ranks to hold Hurley's job—head of the entire state police force. It may well be that, because of his relation to Thomas Kelly, John Kelly had abstained from any involvement in the investigation and arrest and that the unnamed state policeman who did handle the case got some blame for mishandling—possibly because he thought that a light prosecution of his boss's brother would please Sergeant Kelly.

It's interesting to note that immediately after the *Press*'s outraged call for an investigation, *Press* coverage of state police matters seemed to dry up. But within a couple months, stories of police actions began becoming commonplace again. What's more, some of the stories seemed to go out of their way to praise Sergeant Kelly for his work. That was especially the case a year later when Kelly solved the murder of the Topstone hermit (see page 38).

Then there's Roswell Dingee. A popular local house painter, he had been elected a constable for many years. Why did he not intervene or at least arrest Thomas Kelly when he was at the scene? And why did a man who seemed to perform poorly at policing continue to be elected a town constable? The next year, Dingee arrested a man for drunk driving when he was drunk himself (see page 99), and two years earlier, he had shot a man who was fleeing an arrest for a fairly minor offense worth a forty-seven-dollar fine (see page 81).

A BURNED CROSS FOR CHRISTMAS

Another case of bigotry gained national attention and wound up with the prosecution of the bigot in both state and federal courts.

Two nights before Christmas in 1978, Edward Browne, his wife and their two children were baking Christmas cookies and singing carols as they prepared for the holiday. Around midnight, Mrs. Browne noticed a glow coming through a front window of their Old Sib Road home. She looked out and saw a six-foot-high cross burning on their front lawn.

For Mr. Browne, who is black, and his wife, who is white, it was a frightening experience. For Ridgefield, the cross burning shocked a community where only about fifty of its twenty thousand residents were black. It led to years of litigation, including the involvement of a man who is now one of Connecticut's U.S senators.

———————

"We're afraid to go out at night and we're all practically sleeping in the same room," Edward Browne told a reporter two days after the cross burning. He was barricading the doors at night and leaving many lights lit.

Edward Browne examines the cross burned outside his home on Christmas Eve 1978. Ridgefield Press *photo by Larry Fossi, Ridgefield Historical Society archives.*

Browne, who was thirty-five at the time, was an executive recruiter who had moved to town six months earlier. He said the family found Ridgefield charming and the people they met were friendly. And in interviews after the event, he never expressed anger at the community, only at those who had burned the cross. At the outset, he was not even sure of the motive.

"It's easy to say that it is racial because I'm black living in a white neighborhood," he told the *News-Times* in Danbury. "But it could have been a prank. It was a sick person, no matter whether he is black or white. He has a lot of hatred. Not only that, he is a coward."

Ridgefield police began an investigation immediately. But by mid-January 1979, no suspects had been arrested, and the Brownes were becoming anxious.

"Time is running out for the police," Browne said, adding that if the local police didn't act, he might seek state or federal assistance. The cross burning was having "a terrible psychological effect" on his family, he said.

By then, he suspected that an adult was responsible. "I think this is somebody with some hatred and some really ugly motive was behind this," he told the *Hartford Courant* on January 13.

He was right about the hatred and the motive.

On January 24, Police Chief Thomas Rotunda called a press conference to announce the arrest of five young men, ages fifteen to twenty, who were charged with criminal mischief in the third degree and disorderly conduct, both misdemeanors. The five came from Ridgefield, Bethel, Danbury and New Fairfield.

One of the five, a Ridgefield eighteen-year-old, was the self-admitted ringleader of the group. He later told the *Ridgefield Press*, "I hate blacks."

In 1951, Ridgefield had become one of the few towns in Connecticut to have its own chapter of the National Association for the Advancement of Colored People (NAACP). Over the years, the chapter had had as many as two hundred members, most of them white. The chapter was formed to make the community more aware of the existence of a local black community and the problems it faced, including lack of affordable housing. The chapter had been active in the town, usually working behind the scenes to deal with any racial problems. Its members were vocal on many issues, and the chapter was among the first organizations to publicly support a new Ridgefield police headquarters.

William Webb, the chapter's first president, went on to become president of the Connecticut NAACP and a minister.

When the arrests were made, NAACP officials were relieved that an action had been taken but weren't pleased with the charges, which seemed extraordinarily mild for a deed so vile. Bernard Fisher, then president of the Connecticut NAACP, and Webb, still head of the Ridgefield branch, also appeared at the police news conference. While they thanked the police for their work, they criticized the charges.

"All this is, is a slap on the wrist," Fisher said.

NAACP president William Webb, at a press conference, found the arrest charges "rather light." His wife, Delia (*left*), agreed. *Burt Kearns photo,* Ridgefield Press *archives.*

The charges, it turned out, were not selected by the police but by the man who would prosecute them in the Superior Court in Danbury, State's Attorney Walter Flanagan. "They were the charges we felt appropriate to the offense," Flanagan said later.

While police reported the five defendants claimed the cross burning was "just a prank," Browne told the *New York Times*, "I don't consider this to be a prank. I think of it this way: If somebody burns a cross in front of my house, it has a lot of definite meanings. It means 'get out' or something else."

By late February, Browne was reporting harassing phone calls and notes. He estimated the callers were twenty-two to thirty years old and usually threatened to burn down the Brownes' house, told them to get out of town and offered "a lot of profanity, racial jargon, and rhetoric."

"I'm not scared, but it's just a pain, a distraction, and an inconvenience," he told Burt Kearns, a reporter for the *Press*. "It could have been a handful of people out there who are out-and-out racists who decided that they were going to do something about this," he theorized. "The fact that I'm in an interracial marriage is bound to annoy people, and they have the right to think the way they want. But when they take that thinking and start to invade on my privacy, they ought to be dealt with seriously."

"I'm the wrong person to do this to," he added. "I'll find them, and I'll deal with them. They'll be facing federal charges. I've got two-by-fours across the doors, a security system and more lights outside. I'm basically prepared to defend myself."

Was he carrying a gun? Kearns asked.

"I'm prepared for any intruders," he replied.

In April, Browne complained to the office of U.S. attorney Richard Blumenthal, now a U.S. senator from Connecticut, that the cross burning had violated his civil rights under federal law. Blumenthal asked the Federal Bureau of Investigation to look into the case to see if federal charges should be lodged against the five. There had been allegations that the Ku Klux Klan or some similar organization may have been involved, which also prompted a representative of the Department of Housing and Urban Development (HUD) to visit Ridgefield to find out if racial discrimination was being practiced in town.

In May, the ringleader pleaded "no contest" to a charge of disorderly conduct in Superior Court and was sentenced to thirty days in jail on that charge. (He was also sentenced to an additional eight months for reckless endangerment in an unrelated case in which a van he was driving hit a thirteen-year-old pedestrian.) The third-degree criminal mischief charge was dropped.

The twenty-year-old was also sentenced to thirty days. Two seventeen-year-olds were handled as youthful offenders, which meant actions in their cases would not be made public. The fifteen-year-old was turned over to Juvenile Court authorities.

Then in late September, U.S. attorney Blumenthal announced that a federal grand jury had indicted the ringleader, by then nineteen years old, on charges of "intimidating and interfering with a family" by burning a cross in front of their house "because of their race and color, and because they were occupying and enjoying that dwelling." The charges were a violation of U.S. Code 42, the Fair Housing Act, under a subsection that makes it a misdemeanor for anyone who "by force or threat of force willfully injures, intimidates or interferes with, or attempts to injure, intimidate or interfere with any person because of his race, color, religion, sex, handicap…familial status…or national origin and because he is or has been selling, purchasing, renting, financing, occupying, or contracting or negotiating for the sale, purchase, rental, financing or occupation of any dwelling." It was the first time such an action had ever been pressed in Connecticut.

Blumenthal said the federal charge was warranted because of "all the circumstances of the alleged offense…the impact on the Browne family, and the possible deterrent effect of prosecution." He would not comment on why the other four involved in the cross burning were not being prosecuted.

Ben Andrews, executive director of the state NAACP, welcomed the charges. "It's hard to speak in terms of satisfaction with something of this nature, but I think it is appropriate," he said, adding that he was concerned about the increase in racial incidents in the area and noting that Ku Klux Klan literature had recently been distributed in Danbury.

With respect to the cross burning, there was no question about the ringleader's feelings. He described his participation in a June interview with Kearns (who later became a news producer for WNBC-TV and managing editor of the TV shows *Hard Copy* and *A Current Affair*) and fellow *Press* reporter Larry Fossi (now a prominent attorney in New York City).

The nineteen-year-old confessed that he had planned the cross burning because he didn't like having Browne in his neighborhood. "I hate blacks," he said. "I'm prejudiced. I didn't even know that his wife was white until I read it in the paper. I had just seen him around." He had already built the cross that he planned to burn that Halloween at the Brownes' home but dropped the plan because there would be too many people out at night.

According to information Kearns uncovered, four of the five had spent an evening of hard drinking at the Scorpio Lounge in Danbury when the ringleader, complaining about his black neighbor, suggested burning the cross that he had already made. He stopped at his mother's house, siphoned gas from her car, wrapped the wood in rags, drove to the Browne house, soaked the cross and ignited it.

"Flames leapt up four to five feet higher than the top of the six-foot cross," according to a federal court record. "It was a spectacular, frightening sight," the transcript said—so frightening, in fact, that the driver in the group (described as a high school dropout) took off in the car, leaving the ringleader and another boy behind. However, he soon thought better of it and returned to pick the two up.

The case was tried in Federal District Court in Bridgeport in May 1980. On May 19, the jury returned a verdict of guilty. Judge T.F. Gilroy Daly sentenced the ringleader to a year in prison but suspended the imprisonment and placed him on probation for three years, with the condition "that he enter into a vocational training program and an alcohol treatment program under the supervision of the United States Probation Department."

Despite the seeming leniency of the sentence, the ringleader appealed, using a public defender, who argued among other things that the government had failed to prove that the cross burning intended to interfere with the Brownes' federally protected right to occupy their home and that the federal government had been "vindictive" in prosecuting the accused on another misdemeanor charge after the state had already successfully done so.

However, in December of that year, the U.S. Court of Appeals for the Second Circuit affirmed the District Court's decision. Thus, the ringleader had a rare and unsavory claim to fame: he may be the only Ridgefielder ever convicted in two separate courts—state and federal—for one illegal act.

GREEN AND WHITE

When actor-comedian Godfrey Cambridge moved to Buck Hill Road in 1974, he called his new fourteen-room home his "dream house." Within weeks, it was his nightmare. The year that followed was full of charges and counter-charges that made national news.

Raised in Harlem, Cambridge graduated from Hofstra College on Long Island in 1955 and worked as an airplane wing cleaner, judo instructor,

Comedian Godfrey Cambridge outside his Buck Hill Road home in 1974. A few months later, his dream house sparked some bitter battles. Ridgefield Press *archives*.

ambulance driver and cabbie to earn money while trying to break into acting. His first paying role—at fifteen dollars a week—was in a 1956 off-Broadway show in which he played a bartender. By 1961, he had won an Obie for Best Performer for his role in *The Blacks*, Jean Genet's drama about racial hatred.

He soon turned to films, often comedies but also dramas, and appeared in fifteen of them. Once he had made a name for himself, he insisted that his roles depict him "as a man, rather than as a Negro."

Cambridge was drawn to Ridgefield for its schools and its "country" atmosphere. But in March 1975, he took three local real estate agents before the Connecticut Real Estate Commission, charging they had misrepresented the condition of the house they sold him. His most oft-quoted example was the day his foot went through the living room floor. Promised repairs were not done before they moved in, he said. He testified that he paid $125,000 for the house (about $607,000 in 2016 dollars) and then had to sink another $100,000 ($485,000) to bring it up to standard.

Of twelve allegations brought by Cambridge and his wife, the commission dismissed ten. The commission did rule that the house was incorrectly described as having a full basement and that the Cambridges were misled into thinking all the flooring was hardwood. The commission eventually suspended the agents' licenses for sixty days, although the agents vehemently maintained the Cambridges had known part of the house had a half-basement and some rooms had plywood flooring.

Many national news stories portrayed the real estate case as a rich white town against a black newcomer. Cambridge never charged that the complaint involved racial motives. In fact, he told the *New York Times* there were no racial overtones. "Money is where it's at," he said. "Black and white? Forget that. It's green and white."

However, soon after the real estate clash, Cambridge was battling Ridgefield's town government, which maintained that he had erected a chain-link fence too close to the road, creating problems for snow plows. Cambridge said the fence was needed to protect his family from harassment and his property from vandals, but he eventually moved it.

Indeed, all the publicity over the real estate case may have stirred up area racists. Cambridge did charge that, because of racial prejudice, his property had been vandalized, his wife was nearly run off the road in her car and his teenage daughter had been threatened not to attend a school dance. The police investigated but were never able to arrest anyone.

By late 1976, relations between the actor and the town had quieted down. Then, suddenly, on November 29, Cambridge suffered a heart attack and died. He was on the Burbank, California set of an ABC TV film, *Victory at Entebbe*, in which he was playing Ugandan dictator Idi Amin. He was only forty-three.

Newspapers reported Cambridge was often overweight, and it was speculated that his habit of "yo-yo dieting" might have been a factor in his early death. He had weighed some 300 pounds in the early '70s but had lost 170 pounds by the time he bought the Ridgefield house.

Amin himself later declared that Cambridge's death "is a good example of punishment by God" since he was involved in a "fictitious film on the invasion of Uganda by Israel because God knows the invasion was wrong." Amin, who called himself dictator for life, was later overthrown, fled Uganda and died in exile.

Cambridge's family eventually abandoned the Ridgefield house, which was foreclosed by the Money Store in 1979. Even that caused a bit of a stir because the high bid on the place was only $120,000—$5,000 in cash and assumption of the $115,000 mortgage. That was less than half of what the Cambridges had invested in the place and far less than the 1979 appraisal of $160,000.

Chapter 5

GOVERNMENT GONE AWRY

E ven those who govern and police us have their failings, and some wind
up behind bars.

THE BUSTER GETS BUSTED

Roswell L. Dingee proves the old adage about calling a kettle black, especially
if you're potted and a cop.

One Saturday evening in late September 1924, Constable Dingee
was parked along West Lane, watching the occasional cars rolling by
from New York. Suddenly he spotted an Empire State auto operating in
what he considered to be a reckless manner. He pulled it over and told
the driver to go to the state police barracks on East Ridge to be placed
under arrest.

Dingee and five people from the car—two young men and three young
women—soon arrived at the barracks and walked up to the front desk,
where Sergeant John Kelly was on duty.

Dingee told Kelly he wanted both men arrested for driving recklessly.

Both? asked Kelly.

Dingee then confessed that he was not certain which of the two men in
front of him was driving the car, and he wanted to cover both bases.

Kelly told Dingee that he knew nothing of the complaint and that Dingee himself should do the arresting. He also suggested that probably just one man was driving.

So Dingee decided to pinch one of them, a man named William Butler. It was a bad choice.

Dingee then took Butler before Justice Samuel Nicholas, who lived nearby, for arraignment. Butler posted seventy-five-dollar bond but also complained to the justice that he thought Dingee was acting oddly and might, in fact, be intoxicated.

Sergeant Kelly, too, had noticed that Dingee was behaving strangely. After a phone call from Nicholas, Kelly took the constable into custody and brought him to the house of Dr. W.H. Allen, woke up the physician and had him examine Dingee. The doctor said there was no question about it: Dingee was drunk.

Kelly then arrested Dingee for operating a motor vehicle while under the influence of liquor and brought him before Justice Nicholas.

Dingee posted $100 bond.

On Monday in Town Justice Court, Justice Nicholas gave Dingee "a most severe reprimand," the *Ridgefield Press* reported that week. "He told Dingee his actions on Saturday night had brought down on his own head the contempt of the court and the people generally, and that the court was much ashamed of it."

Dingee pleaded guilty and was fined $100 plus $16 costs, but $75 was remitted.

Oddly enough, the conviction did not stop Dingee from testifying in the next case, that of William Butler. But he still had to admit that he did not know whether Butler or the other man in the car was driving.

Butler told the court that, in fact, he was not driving. And the other man had not been told to appear in court, so he was not present.

The court believed Butler and dismissed the charges.

Butler, it turned out, was the son of the head of the police force at the huge U.S. Army Supply Depot in Brooklyn and a nephew of a prominent New York City lawyer. One wonders what phone calls the justice might have gotten from the city before the court session that day.

The banner headline across the top of the front page of the *Press* that week read: "Roswell L. Dingee Makes Arrest; Then Arrested Himself."

The headline was written by *Press* editor David W. Workman, who himself was a Ridgefield constable.

NEWLYWEDS IN THE TOMBS

The story of David Dann and his wife, Susan, reads like an episode from *Downton Abbey*, *Upstairs Downstairs* or some other Edwardian melodrama. Susan, a maid in the home of a rich New York City banker, was accused by her employer of thievery, and thanks to incompetent police, she and her husband were both thrown into Manhattan's notorious "Tombs"

The original "Tombs" is shown in 1896, the same year Susie and David Dann were imprisoned there for ten days. *Library of Congress.*

prison and eventually rescued by a wealthy lawyer and future candidate for governor of Connecticut.

David Dann was born on a Ridgefield farm in 1873, a son of Levi Dann, who was a Civil War veteran and well-respected local citizen. In the summer of 1895, a young Irish woman named Susan Lyons was visiting in Ridgefield and met David, then working as a house painter. They fell in love, and David followed Susie to New York City, where she worked as a servant in the Broad Street home of Maurice B. Wormser, a prominent Manhattan banker. They were married soon after but kept their marriage secret, an arrangement that contributed to their eventual arrest.

On the evening of Saturday, January 18, 1896, Maurice Wormser played host to his brother and his brother's wife. Around 10:00 p.m., as the couple was about to depart, the brother asked to see an evening newspaper, which was in the dining room. "I went into the room to get it and found the silverware drawer open," Wormser later testified in court. "I thought nothing in particular of this, but then at 10:45 two servants saw Susan Dann, who was known as Lyons, a waitress in our employ, in the dining room with a big tray of silver, which she was sorting over. The house was then locked up and the burglar alarm set." The two servants were named Amelia and Minnie.

At eight thirty the next morning, Susan Dann reported to Wormser that the silver had been stolen. "She said she discovered this when she had returned from mass," Wormser testified. However, the cook, a Mrs. Ebert, had told Wormser that Susan was seen admitting the baker at 7:45 a.m. and had also been seen at 7:15 in her nightclothes when Mrs. Ebert had dealt with the milkman. That prompted Wormser to question Susan about how she could have had time to go to Mass.

"She admitted that she had not been to mass, but said that she had an appointment to meet a man. After some further questions, she said the man was her husband, although we thought until then that she was a single woman. She stated that she was married a week ago last Sunday in the Dominican Church."

Since Susan Dann was the last one reported seen with the silverware and the doors were locked overnight, suspicion pointed to her. However, she denied having taken anything. "I put the silver away, as I always did, on

Saturday night," she told a newspaper reporter. "And when I missed it on Sunday morning, I reported it at once to Mr. Wormser."

She admitted lying about going to Mass, however, and had instead gone for a walk with her husband. She said she lied because she did not want Wormser to know she was married until her husband had found work in the city, in case she might lose her job.

"I know they say the house was locked, and that the basement gate was fastened," she said. But when she returned from her early morning meeting with her husband, she found the gate open. "And that was not the first time I have found it open," she said.

She also told a *New York Herald* reporter that Amelia's and Minnie's statements that she was handling the silver late Saturday evening were false.

Adding to the suspicion surrounding the Danns was the fact that Nellie Lyons, Susan's sister, visited the Wormser house Saturday evening. Nellie at first denied she had been there but later admitted she had indeed paid a visit to her sister.

A police captain named Casey of the East Sixty-seventh Street stationhouse headed the investigation. He told a reporter for the *Herald* on January 23 he was "confident he had arrested the persons concerned in the robbery."

The police suspected the Danns in part because of the lies Susan and Nellie told. Detectives used Amelia, the servant, to identify Nellie Lyons as the woman who had visited the house on Saturday and, Amelia maintained, several times in recent months.

Both Susan and David were taken to the precinct stationhouse, where they were questioned and eventually arrested and sent to the city prison, known as the Tombs. (Today's city prison, the fourth edition of the facility, is still nicknamed the Tombs.) Because Nellie had lied about being at Wormser's on Saturday, police arrested her on a charge of complicity in the theft. However, police also suspected her because the house in which she worked as a cook had been robbed by a masked man several weeks earlier after the owner had been put to sleep with chloroform.

Meanwhile, Mrs. Ebert, the Wormser cook, identified David Dann as a man who had come to the house about ten days earlier. Posing as a plumber, she said, he went through various rooms in the place. Though nothing was taken, it was just one more alleged event that was suspicious.

Captain Casey told a *Herald* reporter that "he had been looking up Dann's record, and it was anything but satisfactory in Ridgefield. He has been shifting about from place to place in this city, apparently trying to get work." He maintained that the silver had not been pawned and that "his men would discover it in the possession of the confederates."

Alas, for Casey, that never happened.

———

Word of the arrests quickly reached David's hometown. "It is said in Ridgefield by a good many people that David Dann, who has been under arrest in New York with his wife on a grave criminal charge, has always appeared to be a quiet, inoffensive young man, and people here cannot believe that he would go wrong," the *Ridgefield Press* reported.

Levi Dann, David's father, quickly began seeking support for his son and daughter-in-law. A Catholic, he approached Father Richard Shortell, popular pastor of St. Mary's Parish, who helped gather statements about David's character.

Levi also knew Melbert B. Cary Sr., a prominent New York City attorney who had a palatial residence in Ridgefield. Levi approached Cary about helping his son. Cary wired Father Shortell, saying the imprisonment was "an outrage" and maintaining that he would procure David's release as soon as possible.

Melbert Brinckerhoff Cary was a good man to have on your side. A Princeton graduate who practiced law with a leading Manhattan firm, Cary was also a writer whose books included *The Connecticut Constitution* (1900) and *The Woman Without a Country*. In 1902, Cary ran for Connecticut governor on the Democratic ticket; he had been chairman of the Democratic State Central Committee for several years. He lost to a Meriden Republican but remained a power in Connecticut politics as well as influential in Ridgefield goings-on. He died in 1946 at the age of ninety-three; at the time, he was the oldest living Princeton alumnus.

Levi collected a large number of testimonials from Ridgefielders endorsing his son's good character and turned them over to Cary. "Mr. Cary was zealous in his endeavor to free these innocent persons," the *Press* said.

Cary told the *Times* on January 31, "I have gone through the evidence… and the only way it connects Susie Dann with the silver is through the fact that she had charge of it. The only way her husband is connected with it is

Melbert B. Cary, with a portrait that hung at Flower Fifth Avenue Hospital, got the Danns out of jail. *Courtesy of Cary Stone-Greenstein.*

Melbert B. Cary lived in this West Lane mansion, which he called Wildflower Farm. It burned down in the 1970s. *Postcard in author's collection.*

through the fact that the morning after the robbery, he walked with her in public for an hour. The only connection made between Miss Lyons and the Wormser house is through her visit there the night the theft was committed. Yet our clients were kept in jail ten days. It was simply an outrage."

After those ten days under arrest, the three suspects were "liberated from the Tombs," as the *Press* put it. A grand jury found no evidence to support the arrest of the three.

"The prisoners report the most abusive treatment from the detectives, and say they were placed in the same cells with the foulest criminals," the *Press* said. "Every conceivable effort was made to extort a confession, and the unfortunate victims were subjected to all sorts of indignities."

After their release, Susie Dann discussed her treatment with a reporter from the *New York Times* who described her as "a tall, comely young woman, with a slight Irish accent."

The Sunday she reported the missing silver, she said, she went to the police station, where "Capt. Casey asked me all kinds of questions. He asked me why I had not said anything about being married, and I said it was because my husband was out of work, and I did not want to lose my place until he got work. Then he asked me if I was really married. He also asked me a great many other insulting questions."

That night she went to her husband's boardinghouse room, where "detectives kept coming around and asking me to tell them where the silver was."

Then, on Tuesday night, "Detective Herlihy came up and told me my sister was drunk down in the police court, and that she had said I stole the silver and had told where half of it was. They took my husband and me down to the station that night, and said we wouldn't be detained, and when they got us there, they locked us up. Detectives and the matron came to me about every fifteen minutes and kept asking me insulting questions and telling me I was lying and try to make me confess that I was a thief.

"After our arrest Detective Herlihy went up to my husband's boarding house and told Mrs. Knott [the landlady] that Mr. Wormser would give her $20,000 if she would tell where the silver was."

Susie also described her and her sister's experience in the Tombs. "They put us in with the lowest kind of women. We heard things that were terrible to us, and were compelled to associate with women who were awful. They said things that men would not say."

Melbert Cary not only got the Danns freed from prison but also sued Susie's employer. Cary blamed Wormser for convincing the police that she should be arrested. He sought $20,000 damages (around $575,000 today) for each of the three people imprisoned.

It seems unlikely, however, that much, if any, money was awarded; perhaps there was an out-of-court settlement for a small amount. Four years later, David Dann was working as a janitor. By 1910, he was painting houses in Rye, a town in lower Westchester County, New York, where he and Susan rented a house. They had four children by then.

In 1916, the Danns were back in Manhattan, where David was still painting houses. But by 1918, when he filled out his military draft information, he was in a New York City hospital, suffering from tuberculosis. A month later, David Dann was dead, only forty-five years old.

THE BELOVED EMBEZZLER

Harvey Lown was much loved in town, even during and after his years in prison for embezzling tax dollars. Ridgefield Press *archives.*

Probably no arrest in Ridgefield's history has evoked the outpouring of emotion that surrounded the case of Harvey Lown, a beloved war veteran and native son who had been Ridgefield's tax collector for thirteen years. Even the judge who sent Lown to prison had tears in his eyes when he pronounced the sentence.

When the arrest came in February 1940, "it was as though a bomb had been dropped in our little community," wrote former town historian Richard E. Venus.

Harvey Bishop Lown was the Norman Rockwell picture of the ideal citizen of a small New England town, a man who had risked his life in World War I, owned a successful local business, had led many major organizations in town, had served on the school board and as a state representative and, with his beautiful schoolteacher wife, was invited to many of the nicest social events in Ridgefield.

Born in 1899 in neighboring Wilton, young Harvey Lown came to Ridgefield at the age of three. He attended local schools and Norwalk High School—Ridgefield had no high school back then—and was both a good student and a fine athlete. "He was a great baseball player, an exceptionally good hitter and base runner, and played the outfield with the grace of a Tris Speaker or Joe DiMaggio," recalled Venus. "He had a very pleasing personality and was very easy to like."

After graduating, Lown worked as a clerk in S.D. Keeler's store (where Deborah Ann's Sweet Shoppe is now) until the outbreak of World War I, when he joined the U.S. Navy. Lown served as a storekeeper aboard the USS *Minnesota* and later the USS *Tenadores*, which was transporting troops and war supplies to France. He sailed on seven missions to France, but on the eighth, his military career nearly ended. At midnight on December 28, 1918, the 485-foot *Tenadores* struck rocks in the Bay of Biscay and began sinking. Lown and fellow crewmates drifted in a lifeboat for two days before being rescued by a minesweeper. He was then assigned to a destroyer, which stayed afloat until war's end.

———

Back in his hometown, Lown went to work for Judge George G. Scott, who had an insurance business and was also the town clerk. It was while working under Scott that Lown was introduced to a bookkeeping technique that was to be his downfall. In 1926, he bought Scott's business on Main Street, a bit south of the town hall, and renamed it the Lown Agency.

Lown was becoming increasingly involved in the community, where he eventually became president of the Promoter's Club, precursor of the Lions Club, of which he was also president. He was chairman of the 1939 Building Committee that enlarged Ridgefield High School with an auditorium (now the Ridgefield Playhouse), cafeteria and classrooms. He was active in the Red Cross, the Masons, the American Legion, St. Stephen's Church and various relief efforts during the Great Depression.

In 1927, Lown was elected the town's tax collector, a part-time job held over the generations by the most respected and trustworthy citizens.

At around this time, he was courting a popular Ridgefield teacher, Elizabeth O'Shea (whose sister Isabel, also a teacher, became the first principal of Veterans Park School). Venus described Elizabeth as "very pretty" and "very popular." Harvey and Elizabeth were married in August 1929, two months before the Wall Street crash that was to figure in Harvey's later troubles.

In 1932, Tax Collector Lown was also elected one of Ridgefield's two representatives to the state legislature, another sign of the high esteem in which he was held. A profile of him that year in the *Ridgefield Press* said the tax collector "has given the town a highly efficient administration of that office." It predicted that "as representative to the General Assembly, Mr. Lown will undoubtedly give the same conscientious and efficient performance of the duties as given to those of the past."

Lown's profile in the paper was accompanied by another—that of Judge George G. Scott, with whom Lown had worked and from whom he bought the insurance business. Scott was also a public official, serving among other things as town assessor, judge of probate and town clerk. Lown learned a lot from Scott—including how to deal with money.

According to 1940 notes written in pencil by *Press* publisher and editor Karl S. Nash and found in an old file, "Scott's system of bookkeeping was lax. During his incumbency, [he] kept money of town and money of his business in same pot. That was how Mr. Lown learned the business."

Lown began doing the same thing, keeping his insurance business income in the same account as his tax collections. It simplified his bookkeeping but led to problems.

Ridgefield in the 1930s was suffering from the effects of the Great Depression. Many people were in financial trouble. "We know of several people who went to see Harvey when they were unable to pay either their premiums or their taxes," historian Venus wrote in 1984. "After hearing their plight, he would agree to carry them until they were back on their feet."

To help his insurance customers, Lown started using the town's tax income to cover premiums. He would replace the tax money when he had received enough

Harvey Lown's office was near town hall and just to the left of Ridgefield Hardware (which later moved across Main Street). *1940s postcard in author's collection.*

insurance money to do so. For most of his years in office, Lown was able to cover the premium payments he "borrowed" before there was any problem.

Ridgefield was not alone among Connecticut's 169 towns in having officials who commingled funds. It was apparently a common practice, especially among smaller towns. But the Depression led to shortages in many municipal accounts in the state, and problems became so widespread that in 1939, the General Assembly passed a law requiring regular audits of the books of town offices involved in handling tax dollars.

"It was said that some officials could see the axe about to fall and were successful in getting their houses in order," Venus said. "Several audits were made and failed to disclose any wrongdoing."

In November 1939, the state tax department sent auditors to look at Ridgefield's books. Lown was at the top of his popularity; he'd just been reelected tax collector by a huge margin, and he had recently been chosen president of the Connecticut Tax Collectors Association. One town official told a newspaper, "The audit is simply the first in a routine check-up which in the future will be made at stated periods in accordance with the enactment of the 1939 legislature."

But when the auditors stayed in town hall longer than expected, people began to wonder if something was amiss. And in early December, the state tax department disclosed it had found "irregularities" in Ridgefield's tax collection records.

The *Bridgeport Telegram* reported on January 9, 1940, that a preliminary report on Ridgefield's audit had been turned over to state tax commissioner Charles J. McLaughlin and state's attorney Lorin W. Willis. McLaughlin had ordered the audit when, he said, tax receipts and bank balances over the previous two years "appeared to be out of balance."

Then, on January 16, Lown resigned as tax collector and was immediately arrested for embezzlement.

Ridgefielders couldn't believe what was happening. Much loved in town and much respected throughout Connecticut, Harvey Lown was under arrest, charged with misappropriating funds.

First Selectman Winthrop Rockwell was shaken. The fellow Republican and longtime friend of Lown called an emergency meeting of the Board of Selectmen, the people who run town government.

However, when many citizens and three reporters from local newspapers showed up, Rockwell and his board tried to have them all ejected so the officials could discuss the auditors' report in private. That sparked angry outcries. The reporters and some citizens refused to leave, believing the discussion should be public. Eventually, the meeting was canceled, but the outrage at the attempt at secrecy became so widespread that the selectmen wound up releasing the report to the public.

It turned out that Lown's tax accounts were missing some $11,500—nearly $200,000 in today's dollars.

Lown pleaded guilty. With the help of friends, he also made full restitution of the missing $11,500. Nonetheless, the state wanted to make an example of him so that public officials across Connecticut would heed the new, tough law on commingling tax funds.

Lown was brought before Judge Carl Foster in a packed courtroom at Superior Court, Bridgeport.

First Selectman Rockwell testified on Lown's behalf. "He was a man for whom we always felt there was a great future," he said. "This unfortunate situation would never have occurred had it not been for the fact that he devoted so much of his efforts and time to civic affairs."

Rockwell argued that "it was more than a man's job and if it weren't for this and other civic undertakings which he shouldered and the fact that he had so many friends whom he disliked to dun for insurance premiums in the conduct of his own business, he would never have been in this position."

State's attorney Willis took a different tack, telling the court that because Lown had so many friends among his clients, he was lax in pressing them for premium payments. When it came time for him to send the money to the insurance companies, he "unfortunately fell into the habit of drawing money from the town funds to make good to the companies he represented, but always with the intention of making good, just as every embezzler does." When Lown did collect the late premiums, he would return the money to the town accounts, but he was never able to quite catch up.

Willis argued that Lown had been doing this since he first took office and each year fell further behind until the accumulated shortages reached about $11,500. "We have before us the unhappy situation which has become all too common, of a tax collector in whom the public placed its confidence and held in high esteem, and who then proves faithless," Willis said.

Tax collectors, he said, "fail to realize the gravity of such an offense. It strikes a blow at the orderly forms of democratic government and these things cannot be overlooked. I understand that several townspeople, including officials, are here today to testify in Mr. Lown's behalf, but it is difficult to understand how town officers can take any stand in this matter."

The judge felt he had little choice in the case. His decision prompted an unusually emotional sixty-five-word sentence opening to the news story in the *Bridgeport Post*:

> *One of the most dramatic incidents in the history of the Superior Court, a picture so rare that spectators sat breathless in their seats in stunned silence after it was over, occurred today when Judge Carl Foster, voice choked with emotion and tears flooding his eyes, sentenced Harvey B. Lown, 40, former Ridgefield tax collector, to state's prison for two to five years for embezzlement.*

The judge, the account continued, "seemed nearly carried away by an inner emotional turbulence as he declared, prior to the sentencing: 'This man deserves every ounce of credit, yet the law must be upheld.'"

Judge Foster's sentence shocked most people, both because he'd seemed sympathetic to Lown and because state's attorney Willis had repeatedly referred to the fact that Lown had made full restitution of the losses and always was—and still was—highly regarded by his town.

The sentence was tougher than those handed out today. During his first year in prison, Lown could receive only one letter a week, and his wife was limited to only two thirty-minute visits a month.

"This tragic situation had a profound effect on many people," said Venus. "The person most affected, after Harvey himself, was his ever-loyal wife, Elizabeth, who stepped into the breech and carried on the Lown Insurance business."

Despite his conviction, Lown kept his name on the business. This advertisement is from 1955, twelve years after he was released from prison. *Author's collection.*

In fact, that business continued in operation for many years. Even while Lown was in prison, many Ridgefielders would buy their insurance from his wife. People still loved Lown and tried to help in many ways. Dr. and Mrs. Robert DuBois, for instance, doubled their amount of insurance to show their support for him.

When he was released from prison in 1943, "the strain had taken its toll," Venus said. "The once vibrant and enthusiastic Lowns would never be the happy people they had been."

Nonetheless, Lown remained a part of the business and social community and was particularly active in the American Legion, where he served many years as chairman of the Sailors, Soldiers and Marines Fund, retiring in 1962 because of poor eyesight. In 1964, he was elected president of the Last Man's Club, a group of World War I veterans. In a touch of irony, his vice-president was John C. Kelly, former head of the Connecticut State Police Department.

The Lown Agency was eventually sold to A.J. Carnall, which is now part of the Fairfield County Bank Insurance Services. Elizabeth died in 1959 at the age of fifty-seven. A year later, Lown married Katherine Klein English, a widow from Bethel.

When he died in 1967, the man who had once been a friend of everyone in town and subject of countless front-page stories, good and bad, had only a brief six-paragraph obituary placed deep inside that week's *Press*. It said nothing of his having been the town's tax collector for thirteen years—or of his arrest and imprisonment.

"Harvey's loyal friends have always felt that he never shortchanged anyone but himself," Venus said.

THE CORNEN CRISIS

The American public seems to expect politicians to have a crooked side, but religious leaders tend to be more trusted. Perhaps that's how one Ridgefield church official managed to pocket a sizable amount of money before being caught. The son and grandson of two of the richest men to live in town in the nineteenth century, Cyrus Cornen wound up his relatively brief life as a poor traveling salesman far from home and family.

Cyrus Alexander Cornen Jr. was born in 1878 in the oil fields of Pennsylvania, where his father, Cyrus Cornen, and grandfather Peter P. Cornen, both Ridgefielders, had moved to dig oil wells. Peter was among the earliest oil wildcatters in the United States; he was probably also Ridgefield's first millionaire. He and Henry I. Beers, his brother-in-law, bought a fifty-acre farm in Cherry Run, Pennsylvania, for $2,500. By 1864, the farm was dotted with oil wells. At one point the two rejected an offer of $4 million ($64 million in 2016 dollars) for the farm. Peter Cornen was also a shrewd real estate man; in the 1860s, he acquired sixteen lots in Manhattan. He sold them in 1872 for $65,000 ($1.2 million today). Part of Grand Central Terminal now occupies those lots.

Cyrus Cornen Sr. also made more than $1 million in the Pennsylvania oil fields and, like his father, returned to Ridgefield and lived at the family homestead at the

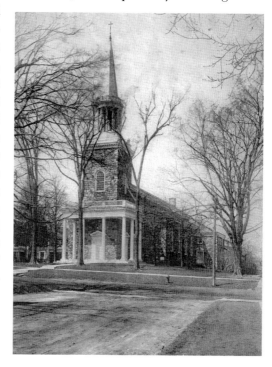

Cyrus Cornen Jr. pocketed donations to the fund that built St. Stephen's Church, shown here in 1915, the year it was completed. *Author's collection.*

corner of Danbury and Farmingville Roads (now the site of the headquarters of Fairfield County Bank, one of whose founders was Peter). Cornen Sr. wrote in 1911 that the estate included "a house large enough for a moderate-sized hotel."

By his twenties, Cyrus A. Cornen Jr. was becoming involved in many aspects of hometown life, serving as master of the Jerusalem Lodge of Masons, a member of the building committee for the new Benjamin Franklin Grammar School (the "old high school" on East Ridge), treasurer of the Ridgefield Electric Company, an officer of the Ridgefield Savings Bank and treasurer of St. Stephen's Church, where he was also on the vestry and his family had been active for years. In 1910, he ran for and was elected town clerk. Around the same time, he was also elected judge of the town's Probate Court.

However, in 1916, suspicions began to arise that not all was going well with Cornen's handing of finances for St. Stephen's Parish.

St. Stephen's had just completed a huge project: the building of a new church, the handsome stone structure that stands today on Main Street in the village. The first service took place in May 1915, but the official consecration ceremony was scheduled for May 1916, led by the Right Reverend Chauncey B. Brewster, bishop of Connecticut. However, a few months before the consecration, the vestry, the committee that oversaw the church's operations, began to notice the church coffers seemed to lack some of the money that had been contributed toward the building project. Bills weren't being paid—and the building had to be free of debt when the consecration took place.

According to records and reports that Robert S. Haight uncovered for his 1975 history of St. Stephen's, the rector and the parish clerk met with Cornen in the early spring of 1916. "From these discussions, it developed that the treasurer had virtually no records to support either expenditures or receipts," Haight said.

A committee was appointed to examine the situation with an accountant. "Surprisingly, considering the condition of the church's finances, Mr. Cornen was reelected treasurer in April 1916. The vestry probably did not yet want to publicize the church's financial situation and was not quite sure that any misappropriation of funds had occurred. By the end of April, however, the bad news was known but the amount of money missing was impossible to establish because of the lack of records, particularly donations to the building fund."

By early May, the church faced an unexpected deficit of $13,000—equivalent of more than $300,000 today.

What Haight called a "whirlwind campaign" was undertaken to pay off the debt. Since St. Stephen's had quite a few wealthy parishioners, the money was quickly collected and debt on the building cleared in time for the consecration ceremony on May 30.

Cornen resigned effective May 26, in time for the ornately printed program for the consecration to list his replacement, Seth Low Pierrepont, as parish treasurer. A millionaire diplomat and naval officer who later donated what's now Pierrepont State Park, Pierrepont probably was largely responsible for getting Cornen's losses covered, both through donations and his own money.

There was extensive coverage of the consecration ceremony in the *Ridgefield Press*, but the leaders of the church were apparently able to keep Cornen's financial misdeeds out of the newspaper. Nor was there any indication about his having taken money from the town through his posts as town clerk and probate judge until more than fifty years later when the

The Consecration
of
St. Stephen's Church
Ridgefield, Conn.
by
The Right Reverend Chauncey B. Brewster, D.D.
Bishop of Connecticut

Tuesday, May the Thirtieth, 1916

✠

Rector
REV. WILLIAM B. LUSK, M.A.

Wardens
W. ANDREW BENEDICT   A. H. STORER

Vestrymen
D. F. BEDIENT   W. J. HUMPHRYS
W. H. BEERS   C. B. NORTHROP
G. E. BENEDICT   S. L. PIERREPONT
THADDEUS CRANE   F. E. STORER
S. L. PIERREPONT, *Treasurer.*   F. E. STORER, *Clerk.*

Building Committee
REV. JOHN H. CHAPMAN

W. ANDREW BENEDICT   E. P. DUTTON
JONATHAN BULKLEY   MISS MARY OLCOTT
WILLIAM BUNKER   MRS. A. H. STORER

The program for the church's consecration shows Seth Low Pierrepont as treasurer. He took over from Cornen, who embezzled donations for the project. *Author's collection.*

Press, then under different management, said he'd reportedly pocketed an undisclosed sum.

If Cornen did also embezzle town funds, how did it go unreported? Speculation is that Cornen's friends and family quickly paid off any missing money and managed to convince the town fathers to keep the whole affair secret. The newspaper's editor and publisher, who may have known something was amiss, was David W. Workman; it is interesting to note that Workman's wife later became clerk of St. Stephen's Parish, serving from 1931 until 1953. Workman himself later became a town constable.

Cyrus Cornen soon left Ridgefield, never to be seen again in the community. He and his wife, Annie Mae, first moved to Pittsburgh, Pennsylvania; his draft registration application from 1918 says he was working as a "motor truck salesman" at a business called Mueller Brothers, perhaps operated by an old family friend from the Cornen family years in the oil fields.

By 1930, he was living in Richmond, Virginia, and three years later, he was in Newport News, working as a traveling salesman. He died

Cyrus Cornen Jr.'s gravestone, a fraction of the size of that of his parents and grandparents, sits far from the family plot. *Author photo.*

The Cornen family plot includes one of the tallest obelisk stones in Ridgefield but doesn't include Cyrus Jr. *Author photo.*

there in 1935 at the age of fifty-one, succumbing to the effects of high blood pressure.

Cyrus's body was shipped back to Ridgefield, where he was buried in the Ridgefield Cemetery. There, the wealthy Cornen family has a gated plot, complete with one of the tallest monuments in any Ridgefield cemetery. But Cyrus is not in the Cornen plot—perhaps a sign of his estrangement from his family. Instead he is buried with his wife's parents, Richard and Roxana Nash Walker. Cyrus's parents and four siblings who died young are all mentioned on the monument; he is not.

After her husband's death, Annie Mae Cornen came back to Ridgefield to live with her sister. Late in life, the two moved to Bradford, Vermont, to live with her sister's daughter. Annie died there in 1958 at the age of eighty-three. Her brief obituary in the *Press* said little about her life but did note she was "the widow of a former Ridgefield town official, Cyrus Cornen."

Chapter 6

THE MYSTERIOUS MISSING

Over the years, missing Ridgefielders have sparked nationwide police manhunts and national headlines. One missing person, for whom Ridgefield was a destination, became a famous millionaire, and another's disappearance helped change law enforcement techniques.

A YOUNG SCHOLAR VANISHES

Nineteen-year-old Ridgefielder Fred Grossfeld was a quiet, scholarly honor student at Massachusetts Institute of Technology, where he was a sophomore majoring in mathematics. He loved books and spent many hours in libraries.

On the evening of November 30, 1965, Fred played bridge with three friends in a dormitory where his own room was located. After the game ended, he said goodnight and left. He was never again seen alive.

When Fred Grossfeld vanished in 1965, a nationwide search was undertaken, largely sparked by his father, who believed foul play was involved. Ridgefield Press *archives*.

It was two days before MIT campus police learned Fred Grossfeld had vanished. Campus police then spent several days either waiting for news or looking into his whereabouts before finally notifying his parents on December 6, nearly a week later.

"We found the delays shocking; the university found them routine," Fred's father, Israel Grossfeld, told MIT's president eight months later. Indeed, when Grossfeld approached an MIT spokesman about publicizing his missing son in the Boston newspapers, he was told, "It isn't a story. Kids disappear every day. This isn't news."

"Then I'll make it a story," Grossfeld shot back.

In the weeks that followed, Grossfeld undertook a tireless campaign to publicize the disappearance of his son, who he believed had been accosted by robbers or was suffering from amnesia. He knocked on doors of police stations, politicians' offices and media newsrooms. Headlines began appearing across the country; the *New York Times* carried at least four stories.

Fred Grossfeld's disappearance was shrouded in mystery. There was no sign of anything amiss. His room was found in perfect condition. Except for an olive-green raincoat, nothing was missing; even his watch was still sitting on his desk.

Grossfeld was described as a "very quiet, studious boy, who spent most of his time reading and studying," the *Ridgefield Press* reported on December 9. "He rarely left the MIT campus. He played chess and Ping Pong in addition to bridge." His father discounted rumors that he was having trouble in school, noting his son had a 4.8 grade point average of a possible 5.0. "His only weak subject was physical education," Israel Grossfeld told the *Times*.

The FBI had briefly investigated in December after Israel received a ransom call from someone demanding $3,000 for Fred's return and telling the father to wait the next day near five pay phones at the corner of Tremont and Boylston Streets in Boston. Grossfeld called authorities, and the next day, Boston police and the FBI staked out the area as Grossfeld waited at the corner. No call came.

Grossfeld said at the time that he believed the caller never contacted him because news of the call and stakeout had appeared in Boston media the night before. "I fear that because I did not follow the caller's advice to not contact the authorities, they might have killed Fred," he said.

When nothing materialized, the FBI dropped out of the case.

However, national law enforcement officials began to take more notice after Israel pursued politicians like U.S. senators Abraham Ribicoff (D-Connecticut) and Ted Kennedy (D-Massachusetts), who in turn pressured U.S. attorney Nicholas Katzenbach to personally review the merits of the case. In early February, Katzenbach wound up ordering the FBI to resume the search for the boy.

A native of Poland who was persecuted as a Jew by the Nazis, Israel Grossfeld had come to this country in 1949 with only eight dollars to his name. He eventually opened I. Grossfeld Ltd., a top-drawer men's clothing store on Main Street.

As he worked to find his son, he virtually walked away from the business. Many people in the community, including an airline pilot and the owner of a competing store, volunteered to work at Grossfeld's shop while the father searched for his son. Scores of Ridgefielders also helped him send thousands of missing-person flyers all over the county—even to hundreds of libraries because Fred had been such a book lover.

"If it takes all of my life, this is my No. 1 job—to find the boy, nothing else," Israel told the *Times*.

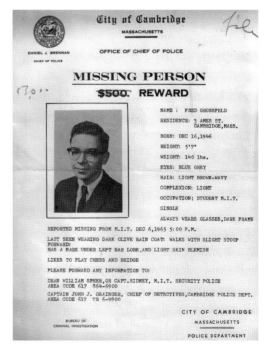

Posters were widely circulated around the country, many by Ridgefield volunteers. The penciled note indicates that the reward amount rose from $500 to $13,000. Ridgefield Press *archives*.

The search came to an end on February 8, 1966. A Beacon Street woman was walking her dog along the Esplanade of the Charles River in Boston when the pet broke loose, ran about fifteen feet out onto the frozen river and began barking. Embedded in the ice was the body of Fred Grossfeld.

Boston police reported that, except for his olive-green raincoat, he was clad entirely in black clothing, including a black shirt and black tie. Investigators found no evidence of foul play.

His father was crushed. He could barely do more than nod his head when he came to the police mortuary to identify the body. He had been in Boston to meet with Cardinal Richard Cushing to enlist his aid in the search campaign.

How did Fred Grossfeld wind up frozen in the Charles River? An autopsy found that the boy had drowned. There was speculation that he had committed suicide by jumping off a bridge over the Charles River, but in a letter to the *Press* on February 15, Israel Grossfeld and his wife, Mina, wrote: "We are sure to our innermost soul that Freddie was not a suicide. He once expressed himself specifically on the subject, saying that only 'sick' people did such a thing. He could not inflict pain on anyone or anything, and certainly not on himself."

Instead, the Grossfelds said, "we believe that Freddie met with foul play, whether from a gang of delinquents roaming the streets or from someone out of the vast hate world we shall probably never know."

The week after the discovery, Israel Grossfeld told the *Press*, "I am not going to let the files be closed. If the police don't care to pursue the case, I will pursue it myself. This is something that I feel I must do for the memory of my boy and for my own peace of mind."

Grossfeld returned to the MIT campus to try to determine whether school and police officials were making any effort to solve the mystery. He was accompanied by author Max Gunther and photographer Joseph Consentino, both Ridgefielders, who had been assigned by the *Saturday Evening Post* magazine to cover the story.

Gunther, who had already spent three days interviewing Fred's dormitory neighbors as well as campus officials, told the *Press* on February 16 that he "found no evidence that Fred was unhappy or worried in the weeks before his disappearance. Furthermore, Fred's friends recalled that the brilliant young scholar had always shunned physical violence and was extremely sensitive to pain, cold and other discomfort.

"If Fred was going to commit suicide," Gunther said, "it seemed unlikely to his friends that he would choose such an agonizing method as jumping into an icy river and drowning."

By the spring of 1966, Israel Grossfeld had recovered enough to focus on a new campaign: the creation of a federal agency handling missing persons.

"We need what a number of other countries already have: A federal bureau for missing persons, under the FBI," Grossfeld wrote Senator Ribicoff in July. "In the areas of taxation, water control, education, and movement of traffic, we have gained immeasurably by the unity and coordination of federal control. Why not in personal safety?"

He had already complained to the MIT president, writing, "It is unfortunate that disappearances of college students are each treated as a common, routine matter. In most cases they probably do present no cause for concern, but this results in tragedy for the few exceptions that do occur." He felt that MIT should have been more diligent in dealing with Fred's disappearance and should have notified area police and the parents immediately. "We shall probably never know whether this entirely usual lack of communication made the difference between life and death," he told the MIT president.

Grossfeld found a supporter in Senator Ribicoff, who had earlier been governor of the state. In 1967, Ribicoff introduced a bill to create a federal office to help local police departments find missing persons. It would, as the *Times* reported, "set up a separate investigative staff within the Justice Department concerned solely with missing persons....The staff would assist directly in investigations if requested to do so by local policemen.... The office would also serve as a national clearinghouse for information on missing persons, using modern computer technology to collect and store information from all over the country."

Such an agency would no doubt be overloaded unless it had thousands of staff members. But the federal government did institute the National Crime Information Center, or NCIC, whose huge databases include not only criminals but also missing and unidentified persons. Today, up to twelve million searches a day are done by law enforcement agencies using NCIC. Many of those are for missing persons.

But as a result of the efforts of Israel Grossfeld and others, other improvements in dealing with missing persons have been made. "Many police departments used to wait 24 to 48 hours before accepting a missing persons report," said current Ridgefield Police chief John Roche. "No more."

Grossfeld had argued that any delay in searching for the missing makes the job tougher. Chief Roche agreed. In Ridgefield and in Connecticut in general, missing persons now get instant attention. "The longer you wait, the less you have the ability to find the person," Chief Roche said. While many missing persons cases may involve miscommunications or domestic spats, "you just don't know," he said.

Ridgefield police even plan for missing persons. One of the more frequent types of missing persons is an Alzheimer's patient, who may wander off and get lost. The department maintains a database of dementia victims, with information voluntarily supplied by caregivers, so that such vital details as photos, physical descriptions and habits can be quickly called up at headquarters.

Israel Grossfeld sold his store in 1980, the same year his wife, Mina, a teacher of Russian, died. He eventually moved to Israel and then to Florida, where he became active in the state chapter of the Friends of Israeli Disabled Veterans. He died in 2013 at the age of ninety-one.

GONE ON A SPREE

Ridgefield had been involved in an earlier, widely publicized missing person mystery, but this one involved a fifty-year-old man who vanished in Louisiana.

Daniel Milford, an engineering executive who lived in Ridgefield, had gone to Baton Rouge in August 1951 to supervise the $15-million expansion of an industrial plant. On December 22 that year, he suddenly dropped from sight, reportedly after losing more than $1,400 at gambling tables in Baton Rouge. Police said the last person known to see him alive was a waitress who had given him a ride.

A nationwide manhunt was undertaken.

However, his ex-wife eventually told police that Milford had occasionally "gone on sprees" in the past, sometimes disappearing for months.

Then, in mid-February, Milford called his second wife from Los Angeles, maintaining that his disappearance had been caused by "mental exhaustion" and a "near case of amnesia," family members said.

In a strange ending, Milford was on his way back to Ridgefield with his wife on February 18 when he suffered a heart attack and died in Reno, Nevada.

His brother-in-law told reporters that Milford had been ill ever since he had disappeared. "He had been working too hard and the job had just about knocked him out," he said. "He lost 40 pounds and his heart was bad. He hardly knew what he was doing."

THE RUNAWAY MILLIONAIRE

Most of the newsworthy missing here have been Ridgefielders who disappeared. In one unusual case, Ridgefield was the destination for a missing teenager. And he turned out to be a most unusual runaway.

In May 1944, the sixteen-year-old boy packed a suitcase and, with forty dollars in his pocket, disappeared from his home in Brooklyn, New York. A month later, he was found mucking stalls on a farm in Ridgefield.

It was just the first grand adventure for Jack R. Dick, who would become a millionaire many times over, amass a world-class art collection, acquire a mansion that was once the home of the man who owned the New York Yankees and be arrested for grand larceny and forgery.

How did a Brooklyn teenager wind up cleaning barns and shearing sheep on a Ridgebury farm? Dick would later tell friends that he was a city boy who had always yearned for the country—a white farmhouse amid acres of green fields and rolling hills. He found that "dream" at the farm of William C. Browning, who owned a sizable spread along Spring Valley and Mopus Bridge Roads.

Asking for a job, Dick told Browning he had come from Kansas, where his parents had been killed in a car crash. At five feet, eleven inches, the

Runaway Jack R. Dick mucked stalls at this Ridgebury farm. He later became a multimillionaire. *Old town assessor's photos, courtesy of Ridgefield Historical Society.*

175-pound teenager could, as his father put it, readily pass for several years older than his age. He was hired at twenty-five dollars a month.

Dick's parents apparently understood their son's wanderlust and had done little when he left home. But by June 11, they were getting anxious. His grandmother was ill, and they had heard no word. As Dick later told it, an aunt with show-business connections convinced Walter Winchell to run a missing person's picture in his widely circulated celebrity column, leading to Dick's discovery.

That may have been just a tall tale by a man who was known to be fleet of tongue. In fact, the *New York Times* ran a picture and story on Sunday, June 11. As the newspaper reported the next day, Ridgefield "villagers recognized a photograph of the youth that appeared…in *The New York Times* and when Mr. Browning asked Dick about it, he admitted his identity." His father, Samuel H. Dick, president of a clothing manufacturing company in Manhattan, drove out to pick up his son.

It would not be the wanderer's last stay in Fairfield County.

Jack R. Dick returned to a somewhat normal life in Brooklyn. He was fullback on his high school football team and was named "Most Likely to Succeed" in his yearbook, of which he was editor. But his talent for making money began to show itself at Syracuse University, where, besides attending classes, he ran a mail-order military surplus business and hosted bridge games that involved wagering.

"Bridge was my most remunerative enterprise," he told an interviewer. "My partner and I were very successful at spreading the wealth around, taking from those who were getting more money from home and dividing it up among the less fortunate, namely ourselves. Those were my only Marxist tendencies."

Dick maintained that he left Syracuse without ever graduating but with a $15,000 profit.

After spending seven years working as an executive in a kitchenware business owned by his father, Dick decided in 1958 to strike off on his own in the world of high finance. He said that he began with $25,000 and within a year was worth $12 million—on paper. Then the Securities and Exchange Commission charged him with "kiting"—ordering stock he did not plan to pay for, hoping that he could sell the shares at a profit if they increased in price before the deadline for payment. The SEC in 1960 banned him from various kinds of trading on the New York Stock Exchange, and brokerage houses sued him to recover their losses.

He was so broke, he said, that he had to walk five miles from his posh upper Manhattan apartment to his lawyer's downtown office because he couldn't afford a subway ride. He wound up selling a collection of antique postage stamps for $750,000 to pay off debts.

According to his own account, he spent six months putting his life back in order and looking for a new way to make money. Perhaps recalling his experience at Browning's farm in Ridgefield, he decided to pursue cattle farming. He used his sales skills and business acumen to convince enough investors—including singers Steve Lawrence and Eydie Gorme and actor E.G. Marshall—to back his $350,000 purchase of a 650-acre farm in Wappingers Falls, New York, from Everett Crosby, brother of crooner

Bing Crosby. There he established Black Watch Farms, raising and selling Black Angus cattle. Sales in 1962 were $40,000; six years later, they were $30 million.

Flush with money, Dick returned to his hobby of collecting antiques but focused especially on paintings of English sporting and hunting scenes— riding to the hounds and such—from the eighteenth and nineteenth centuries. Over five years, he scoured the English countryside and participated in countless auctions, amassing what he called "the finest collection of English sporting paintings ever assembled."

"They say I raped England," he said, "and in a way I did," bringing the art to the United States "before anyone knew what was happening." The collection was said to be worth $15 million in 1974—more than $28 million in today's dollars, according to a *Sports Illustrated* profile on Dick and his paintings called "He Took the British for a Ride."

At the age of forty, Dick found that the long hours of turning a farm into a multimillion-dollar business were wearing on him. He had a wife, Lynda, and two children but hardly had time to spend with them. He decided to retire and sold Black Watch Farms to a trucking company looking to diversify. The price was $21.4 million, but he took most of the payment in stock. It was then that he returned to Connecticut, buying a twenty-eight-room mansion on twenty-six acres in Greenwich, atop a ridge with sweeping views of Long Island Sound.

Dunnellen Hall was no ordinary mansion. "This house is like the Hope Diamond," Lynda Dick once told a friend. "It has brought bad luck to everyone who owned it."

Built in 1918 by an industrial magnate, the house was later the home of his grandson, Dan Topping, owner of the New York Yankees. Skater Sonja Henie and actress Lana Turner lived there when they were married to members of the Topping family. It was subsequently owned by an industrialist who ran into financial troubles and by Gregg Sherwood Dodge Moran, a showgirl and former wife of an heir to the

Dodge automobile fortune; her husband, a former New York City cop, killed himself. Another owner, Ravi Tikkoo, an Indian-born supertanker tycoon, also ran into financial troubles and had to sell the place in 1983.

The buyers were Harry and Leona Helmsley, the former the owner of the Empire State Building and other lucrative properties and the latter dubbed the "Queen of Mean." The Helmsleys were subsequently charged with tax fraud; she went to prison for eighteen months while he, too frail for imprisonment, stayed home and died, leaving a $5.5 billion estate to his wife. Ironically, in 1968, the house had been used to film *A Lovely Way to Die*, a drama starring Kirk Douglas and Eli Wallach.

In between Moran and Tikkoo were the Dicks, and their time in Dunnellen Hall was not the happiest. The movie title was perhaps appropriate for Jack Dick, too.

———

Dick wanted Dunnellen as a showplace for his collection of English sporting paintings and other antiques. The walls were covered with his art collection. But it wasn't long before Dick had to look on his art not as private museum pieces but as a means of survival. And some of those paintings may have led to his downfall.

In 1971, Black Watch Farms went bankrupt. Black Watch's owners claimed Dick had misrepresented the company's financial condition and sued him. Dick sued back, charging Black Watch's owners with mismanagement.

Then, the same year, the government joined the fray. A grand jury indicted Dick, and he was arrested by the Manhattan district attorney's office for stealing $840,000 by using false financial statements, forged art gallery invoices and securities he didn't own as collateral to gain a loan to buy more English hunting art, the *New York Times* reported. He was charged with grand larceny, forgery and other counts.

And if all that wasn't enough, Dick's own father and one-time business partner sued his son, and Dick countersued his father in a case appropriately yet colorfully called *Dick v. Dick*. Samuel Dick said Jack failed to live up to a contract between the two and had cheated the father out of millions of dollars, according to Connecticut Supreme Court records. Dad sought $20 million in damages.

Testimony in court revealed that both father and son took part in fraudulent dealings during and after the time they worked together. For instance, Samuel Dick borrowed large sums of money against inventory that did not exist. An employee testified that, in 1956, Samuel ordered him to build a false pile of plywood that had the appearance of being a solid mass but that actually consisted of a hollow cavern surrounded by a small amount of plywood. The worker built the false pile of plywood "so as to create the impression of an enormous pile which was used by the plaintiff as inventory against which moneys were borrowed," court documents said.

Faced with mounting legal costs and virtually no income, Dick was forced to begin selling his cherished collection of English paintings and to put Dunnellen up for sale.

However, his legal and fiscal woes may have also taken their toll on his health. On January 6, 1974, after an evening at a private club in Manhattan, Jack and Betty Dick were being driven to Dunnellen in a limousine when he suffered a massive heart attack and died. He was only forty-five years old.

———

Because of his death, Dick was never tried on the larceny and forgery charges. But he had always maintained his innocence. "I never borrowed or received 10 cents improperly, and I defy anyone to prove that I did," he was once quoted as saying.

To pay off his debts, his prized art collection was shipped to Sotheby's in England, where it sold in three auctions. One painting alone fetched nearly $1 million. The collection Dick considered "the greatest achievement of my life" had, for the most part, returned to its native land.

BIBLIOGRAPHY

Ables, Kay, et al. *A View from the Inn: The Journal of Anna Marie Resseguie 1851–1867*. Ridgefield, CT: Keeler Tavern Preservation Society, Inc., 1993.

Bedini, Silvio A. *Ridgefield in Review*. Ridgefield, CT: 250th Anniversary Committee, 1958.

Biagiotti, Aldo. *Impact: The Historical Account of the Italian Immigrants of Ridgefield, Connecticut*. Ridgefield, CT: Romald Press, 1990.

Bloom, Stephen G. *Tears of Mermaids: The Secret Story of Pearls*. New York: St. Martin's Press, 2009.

Connecticut Education Association. *Responsible Academic Freedom: Challenge to Ridgefield*. Hartford, CT, 1973.

Dilnot, George. *Triumphs of Detection: A Book about Detectives*. London: Houghton Mifflin, 1929.

Haight, Robert S. *St. Stephen's Church, Ridgefield, Connecticut: Its History for 250 Years*. Ridgefield, CT, 1975.

Jordan, Alvin R., et al. *A History of the Town of Lewisboro*. South Salem, NY: Lewisboro History Book Committee, 1981.

Kennedy, Ray. "He Took the British for a Ride." *Sports Illustrated*, June 3, 1974.

Land Records and Vital Records, Town of Ridgefield, 1708–1925.

New York Times.

Ridgefield Press.

Rockwell, George L. *The History of Ridgefield, Connecticut*. Ridgefield, CT: privately printed by the author, 1927.

Venus, Richard E. *Dick's Dispatch: Stories of Ridgefield People and Places*. Copies of 366 articles appearing in the *Ridgefield Press*, 1982–89. Ridgefield, CT: Ridgefield Archives Committee, 1996

Index

ABOUT THE AUTHOR

A Connecticut native and Holy Cross College graduate, Jack Sanders retired in 2014 after more than forty-five years as an editor of the *Ridgefield Press*, for which he has written hundreds of historical articles. His books of history and natural history include *Hidden History of Ridgefield* and *Ridgefield Chronicles* (both The History Press), *Ridgefield 1900–1950* (Arcadia), *Five Village Walks* (Ridgefield Historical Society), *The Secrets of Wildflowers* (Lyons) and *Hedgemaids and Fairy Candles* (McGraw-Hill). He and his wife, Sally, also a newspaper editor, live in a 250-year-old farmhouse in Ridgefield, enjoy bicycling and have two sons and a granddaughter.

Photo by Hildegard Grob.

Visit us at
www.historypress.net

···

This title is also available as an e-book